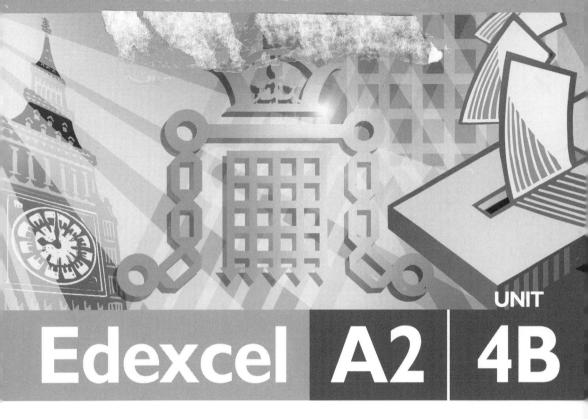

Edexcel | A2 | UNIT 4B

Government & Politics

Other Ideological Traditions

Barry Pavier

Series Editor: Eric Magee

Philip Allan Updates, an imprint of Hodder Education, an Hachette UK company, Market Place, Deddington, Oxfordshire OX15 OSE

Orders

Bookpoint Ltd, 130 Milton Park, Abingdon, Oxfordshire OX14 4SB
tel: 01235 827720
fax: 01235 400454
e-mail: uk.orders@bookpoint.co.uk
Lines are open 9.00 a.m.–5.00 p.m., Monday to Saturday, with a 24-hour message answering service. You can also order through the Philip Allan Updates website: www.philipallan.co.uk

Philip Allan Updates 2009

ISBN 978-0-340-98711-7

First printed 2009
Impression number 5 4 3 2 1
Year 2013 2012 2011 2010 2009

This guide has been written specifically to support students preparing for the Edexcel A2 Government & Politics Unit 4B examination. The content has been neither approved nor endorsed by Edexcel and remains the sole responsibility of the author.

Typeset by Phoenix Photosetting, Chatham, Kent
Printed by MPG Books, Bodmin

Hachette UK's policy is to use papers that are natural, renewable and recyclable products and made from wood grown in sustainable forests. The logging and manufacturing processes are expected to conform to the environmental regulations of the country of origin.

Contents

■ ■ ■

Questions and Answers

Introduction

The Edexcel Advanced GCE (A2) in Government and Politics is a two-unit course. This guide to Unit 4B, Other Ideological Traditions, has been written to help you prepare more effectively for the unit test. It provides an outline of the structure of the unit, guidance on all aspects of the content, examples of questions and answers with examiner comments and advice on how the mark scheme works. Unit 3B, Introducing Political Ideologies, is covered in a separate guide.

Unit 4B focuses on four ideologies: nationalism, feminism, ecologism and multiculturalism. You need to know:
- the core ideas, doctrines and theories that distinguish each ideology from the others
- the ways in which the ideologies may have influenced each other
- the nature and extent of disagreements within each ideology
- how each ideology has changed over time to remain relevant

You also need to know about the differing views of, and tensions within, each ideology as outlined below.
- **Nationalism**: between the different types of nationalism (liberal, conservative, expansionist and anti-colonial) and the ways in which they have manifested politically.
- **Feminism**: between liberal, socialist/Marxist and radical feminism, and anti-feminist theories.
- **Ecologism**: between conservative authoritarian ecologism, eco-socialism, eco-anarchism and eco-feminism.
- **Multiculturalism**: between liberal, pluralist and cosmopolitan multiculturalism, and ideological criticisms of multiculturalism.

How to use this guide

The guide is divided into three sections.
- The **Introduction** sets out the aims of the guide, the details of the unit specification, and the skills required for studying the unit and preparing for the unit test.
- The **Content Guidance** section explains the key concepts and issues in each part of the specification in detail. The coverage follows the outline of the specification.
- The **Questions and Answers** section contains a selection of Unit 4B-style questions. Answers of varying length and quality are provided, each with a commentary indicating the strengths and weaknesses of the response designed to help you to understand precisely what examiners are looking for.

The unit at a glance

Each of the ideologies has to be studied in relation to a number of key concepts. These are ideas that are fundamental to the particular ideology. You need to know not only the definitions of each individual concept but also how they relate to each other and contribute to the ideology's attitude towards wider issues.

Nationalism

Key concepts	Content explanation
• Nation • Nation-state • Tacialism • Patriotism • National self-determination	• A knowledge of the core ideas, doctrines, and theories of nationalism and of the variety of nationalist traditions and their different political manifestations • An understanding of the different types of nationalism and the extent to which nationalism relates to other ideological traditions

Feminism

Key concepts	Content explanation
• Sex/gender • Gender equality • Patriarchy • Public/private divide • Essentialism	• A knowledge of the core ideas, doctrines, and theories of feminist thought, of tensions within feminism and of competing feminist traditions, notably an understanding of the distinctive features of liberal feminism, socialist/Marxist feminism and radical feminism, and also taking into account more recent developments

Ecologism

Key concepts	Content explanation
• Ecology • 'Hard/soft' ecology • Deep/shallow ecology • Environmentalism • Holism • Sustainability • Industrialism • Social ecology • Anthropocentrism	• A knowledge of the core ideas, doctrines, and theories of ecological and environmentalist thinking • An understanding of the range of ecological traditions, and differences between them, focusing in particular on conservative/authoritarian ecologism, eco-socialism, eco-anarchism and eco-feminism

Multiculturalism

Key concepts	Content explanation
• **Communitarianism** • **Post-colonialism** • **Identity politics** • **Minority rights** • **Toleration** • **Diversity** • **Pluralism** • **Cosmopolitanism**	• A knowledge of core ideas, doctrines, and theories of multiculturalist political thinking, and an understanding of the range of multiculturalist views and their relationship to political stances such as liberalism, pluralism and cosmopolitanism • A critical understanding should also be demonstrated of the effectiveness of multiculturalism in ensuring political stability and inclusion, including critiques of multiculturalism

Each of these concepts is explained separately in the Content Guidance section. Their relationship to key issues is also covered.

Examination skills

Your answers in the unit test will be marked according to three common assessment objectives. Each assessment objective is given a weighting. At A2, 50% is allocated to analysis and evaluation (AO2), 30% to knowledge and understanding (AO1) and 20% to communication (AO3). This means that while you need to be able to demonstrate knowledge (AO1) and communicate your ideas clearly (AO3) most emphasis is placed on your ability to analyse and evaluate (AO2).

AO1	Demonstrate knowledge and understanding of relevant institutions, processes, political concepts, theories ands debates.	30%
AO2	Analyse and evaluate political information, arguments and explanations, and identify parallels, connections, similarities and differences between aspects of the political systems studied.	50%
AO3	Construct and communicate coherent arguments making use of a range of appropriate political vocabulary.	20%

Your Edexcel Unit 4 answers will be marked according to these assessment objectives. Remember that you will not just be given an overall mark out of 15 for each of your three short-answer questions and 45 for your essay question — in each answer marks will be given for each assessment objective in the proportions shown above. The total for each question will be a total of the separate marks for each of AO1, AO2 and AO3.

- Short-answer questions:

AO1 = 5 marks

AO2 = 7 marks

AO3 = 3 marks

Total = 15 marks

- Essay questions:
AO1 = 12 marks
AO2 = 24 marks (includes 12 marks for synopticity)
AO3 = 9 marks

Total = 45 marks

In order to get the best possible mark you need to take a few essential steps:
- Understand the question. Focus on command words (e.g. *analyse, evaluate, discuss, identify*) and do what they say. Short-answer questions will be more focused on knowledge and understanding of key concepts. Essay questions require you to make a judgement, signalled by command words such as *'how far'* and *'to what extent'*.
- Answer all aspects of the question. If the question asks 'How and why...' you must give significant space to both of these (at least 30% to each).
- Use examples to support each point you make. As many as possible of these should be contemporary. This shows that you really understand the point you have made and have not simply reproduced a memorised list from a textbook.
- Use correct and precise political vocabulary. This is not only because 20% of marks are now specifically allocated for AO3; correct terminology allows you to make points with clarity and precision. It saves you precious writing time in examinations and makes your point absolutely clear to the examiner.

In addition to assessment objectives, there are performance descriptors for answers on the A/B and E/U grade boundaries. They give you a good idea of what is required to produce a top-grade answer (see the table opposite). You may find it useful to check your practice answers against these criteria, especially in relation to AO3, which is where many otherwise excellent answers frequently lose out. In fact, if you have written your answer so that you meet the A/B level requirements for AO3, it is likely that you will have met them for AO1 and AO2 as well.

Synopticity

In the essay questions 12 of the 24 marks for AO2 are for 'synopticity'. Synopticity means learning to develop an all-round, integrated understanding of the subject.

Synoptic skills involve:
- the ability to identify alternative viewpoints or perspectives on an issue or question
- an awareness of the nature and extent of rivalry between these viewpoints
- an awareness of the significance of the viewpoints for an understanding of the issue or question

In this unit you will achieve synopticity by showing your ability to demonstrate how political ideologies shape political argument and understanding. This can be done in two ways: by understanding how the ideologies differ on crucial issues, such as

Grade boundary	AO1	AO2	AO3
A/B boundary	Candidates characteristically: • demonstrate accurate, detailed and comprehensive knowledge of political institutions and processes, and a competent understanding of political concepts, theories and debates, incorporating the relevant specification content • produce answers that fully address the requirements of the question • demonstrate good contextual awareness • provide accurate evidence and, where appropriate, contemporary examples deployed to illustrate points made	Candidates characteristically: • provide analysis that synthesises political concepts, theories and issues • evaluate political information clearly and fully, using appropriate evidence that may be drawn from the whole specification • make effective comparisons, explaining parallels, connections, similarities and differences	Candidates characteristically: • construct and communicate cogent and coherent arguments and explanations • illustrate a clear sense of direction and, where appropriate, culminate in a coherent conclusion which flows from discussion • use a range of relevant and appropriate political vocabulary
E/U boundary	Candidates characteristically: • demonstrate an outline knowledge and understanding of political institutions and processes, political concepts, theories and debates, with evidence of some relevant specification content • make a limited attempt at answering the question • demonstrate some basic contextual awareness • provide some relevant evidence or examples	Candidates characteristically: • offer limited analysis that shows some awareness of differing ideas • attempt a simple evaluation of political institutions, processes, behaviour, arguments or explanations, and make some comparisons • outline basic concepts and theories • demonstrate some recognition of basic parallels and connections or similarities and differences	Candidates characteristically: • construct and communicate some arguments and explanations with a structure that is narrative or descriptive • illustrate a sense of direction and, where appropriate, offer a conclusion, though relationship with the preceding discussion may be tenuous or implicit • use some relevant evidence and some appropriate political vocabulary

society, human nature and the state and how there are fundamental differences within each ideology over central beliefs and values.

To achieve this you will have to draw on your learning from the AS modules. For instance, in Unit 1 you will have learned about policy differences between the main parties in such areas as environmental policy, social inclusion and equal opportunities. You will be able to use this knowledge and understanding to assist you in the study of ecologism, feminism and multiculturalism.

In Unit 2, you learned about a number of topics such as devolution, federalism, and civil liberties, which will be the starting point for a study of nationalism, feminism and multiculturalism. This will constitute part of your study for the A2 units and provide the basis for more sophisticated analysis and evaluation.

About the exam

Scheme of assessment

The unit test is 1 hour 30 minutes long and each unit accounts for 50% of the A2 mark (25% of the overall mark).

Exam format

Exam type	Written
Duration	1 hour 30 minutes
Question choice	Section A: three questions from a choice of five
	Section B: one question from a choice of three
Question format	Section A: each short-answer question is worth 15 marks
	Section B: each essay question is worth 45 marks
Question focus	Section A: each question relates to concepts linked to a specific ideology
	Section B: each question relates to a key issue related to a specific ideology
Total marks available	90
Overall weighting	50% of total A2 mark (25% of total A level mark)

Timing

Since the two sections carry the same number of marks, it is recommended that you spend 45 minutes on Section A (15 minutes for each question), and 45 minutes on Section B.

How to write good answers

Short-answer questions

You will have to answer three from a list of five questions. This means that there will be a question on each of the four ideologies covered in this unit. One of them will have two questions. There is no guarantee that there will be strict rotation as to which ideology will be examined by two questions.

The questions aim to test your understanding of the basic concepts of each ideology. The command words will be 'why', 'explain' or 'what'. They may also test your ability to compare and contrast the views of two different ideologies on a specific concept. Make sure you do the following:

- Provide a clear definition of the concept.
- Identify two or three main points and then develop them. You may refer to specific individuals who have written about the topic, but do not namedrop just for the sake of it. Use examples to support your argument.
- Make sure that you mention any different opinions on concepts and issues relevant to the question between the various sub-traditions of the ideology (liberal nationalism, radical feminism etc.).
- If there are two command words (such as 'how and why'), make sure that you give them equal treatment.
- Remember that there are more marks allocated for analysis and evaluation (7) than for knowledge (5), and balance your answer accordingly.
- Plan your answers with care. Since you will have only about 15 minutes to write each of the answers to this type of question, you must not get carried away in lengthy but unnecessary detail. You can write a fully comprehensive answer within about 250 words.

Do not answer questions in reverse order by attempting the essay question before the short answers. The short-answer questions prepare you for the essay question. Candidates who attempt to reverse the order usually end up disadvantaging themselves, and the final short-answer question may end up as a hurried afterthought.

Essay questions

You are required to answer one question from a list of three. This means that one ideology will not be covered by an essay question. It is likely — but *not* guaranteed — that the ideology that 'misses' an essay question will be the one which has two short-answer questions.

- Read the question carefully and make sure you answer that question and only that question.
- Take an essay-style approach, which requires an introduction, an argument and a conclusion.
- The main skill tested is AO2 — evaluation.
- There is no 'right' or 'wrong' answer. You will gain marks for the quality of your argument and conclusion.
- You will be required to evaluate arguments, presenting different points of view to allow synopticity to be addressed. Remember that 12 of the 24 AO2 marks are for synopticity.
- Your introduction should provide a clear definition of key terms used in the question. Make it clear that you understand the 'point' of the question and outline the argument you intend to develop in the main body of your essay.
- In the argument section of your essay you should make points in a clear sequence, supporting each with appropriate evidence and qualifying where necessary by use of words such as 'however'.
- Your conclusion should be a new paragraph beginning 'In conclusion...'. Then, clearly and briefly, outline the key points that support your conclusion.

Revision and examination preparation

There is no one single effective method of studying, and of revising and preparing for an examination. To give yourself the greatest chance of success you should prepare systematically.

To do this you need to know:
- the key concepts and content explanation for each of the four ideologies
- the number of questions on the paper
- the different types of question (e.g. short-answer and essay questions)
- how much choice you have (e.g. how many short-answer questions and how many essays you have to answer)
- how much time you have to devote to each question
- the specific demands of each type of question

The later sections of this guide will go over each of these points in detail. Your teacher may well have already provided you with the details of the specification. You can also find this on the Edexcel website (**www.edexcel.org.uk**), together with sample examination questions and the new-style mark scheme. This is important as it provides you with a guide as to what is required to gain the highest marks.

Further pointers for study
- Make sure that you have made notes on each of the concepts and on all the core content. If you have not, you run the risk of being confronted by a question that

you cannot answer. This may then result in you falling into one of the most common examination errors: writing down everything you know about a subject in the hope that something will be relevant. The best way to avoid this is to have done all the hard work before you reach the revision stage. Make sure that you have covered everything, using the specification as a checklist.

- Keep your notes in a folder and in good order. Without this, all the work that you have done will be next to useless and you will not be able to recall the knowledge gained over the preceding months. If there are gaps in your coverage of the specification, then make filling them in your priority. Your teacher may well have provided material about them in hard copy or electronic form.

- One method of learning that is especially useful in revision is to work in small groups or teams with your fellow students. It makes it much easier to fill in gaps — if you have missed a session, others may be able to fill you in on the details. Discussion with others generally leads to greater understanding, as it drives you to clarify your ideas. Another advantage is that some people may have come across new sources (magazine articles, books or internet references) that are relevant to a particular issue. Most importantly, the process of discussion means that you are no longer facing a problem alone and this enables you to hear other people's ideas, which may in turn produce new ideas of your own. If your school or college runs Moodle there may well be an online discussion group facility, where you can raise problems with other students or your teacher.

- Be careful how you use the internet. It is an incredibly useful additional tool to academic study and can be of great value. However, you must not use it as a sole tool. This is especially true for politics as the internet has become the natural habitat of the polemicist, the obsessive and the conspiracy theorist. Some of the information on the internet is wrong and it is not always easy to know what is accurate and what is not.

- On the other hand, there is much valuable material available on the internet that would take you a long time to find otherwise. You need to develop and use your analytical abilities to avoid the pitfalls of internet research. Look for references that you are able to check. Look for internal coherence in the arguments. If statements are based on comments such as 'must be', 'it is obvious that', or 'in all probability', it usually means that there is no evidence.

- When revising, be systematic and follow a clearly worked-out plan. Haphazard, last-minute reading through all your notes is not a good idea.

- Practise answering questions under examination conditions and make essay plans for other questions, including both short-answer and essay questions.

- **Do not** question spot. There is no guarantee of any particular rotation of questions. Many candidates have been badly caught out by thinking that they can second guess the examiner.

- Make sure that you **answer the question that is set**, not one that you may have revised. Taking this approach is another of the most common reasons why many students underperform in examinations. The point of thorough revision is that you prepare yourself to deal with any question that is set.

Remember, examinations are not designed to trap you — they are there to assess how well you can cope with the demands of the specification. If you feel confident that you understand everything in the specification, then you have prepared yourself well.

Content
Guidance

This section of the guide explains what you need to know about the four ideologies studied in this unit: nationalism, feminism, ecologism and multiculturalism

While it is obviously impossible to provide an answer to every question you may be faced with, this section sets out clearly what you need to know and understand about each of the ideologies.

You should pay particular attention to four key issues:
- the core features of each ideological tradition
- the ways in which the ideologies influence each other
- the disagreements within each ideology
- the changing nature of each of the ideological traditions as they adapt to new conditions and attempt to retain relevance

Nationalism

Nationalism in its modern form is a product of the Enlightenment. The concept of 'nation' was central to the French Revolution (1789–99); it was counterposed to the concept of dynasty as the legitimate basis for a state. As such, nationalism was one of the founding principles of liberalism. A crucial question was, however, immediately posed: how do you identify who is part of any particular nation?

Despite liberal theory, nations were not neatly defined homogenous units. Populations were not arranged in perfectly delineated areas, as many units of territory had been exchanged between states at frequent intervals and this had produced significant population movements. This process had created a complex patchwork of populations across Europe, and in other parts of the world as well.

As a result, once nationalism became an influential ideology bitter competition for territory and people emerged. At this point nationalism developed its 'dual' nature. The attempt to force reluctant groups of people into a national unit that they did not desire to join enabled conservative forces to embrace nationalism as a way to mobilise support for the authority of existing states.

Nationalism made an unwelcome return to the centre of European affairs in the 1990s. The collapse of the Soviet Union in 1990–92 took the form of an upsurge in nationalism. The USSR was replaced by 13 states constructed on the 'national principle'. In 1991–92 Yugoslavia disintegrated into a series of civil wars, fought out on the basis of competing nationalisms.

In January 1993 there was a peaceful partition of Czechoslovakia into two states: the Czech and Slovak republics. In this case the two new states were ethnically and linguistically close to each other, to the same extent as are England and (lowland) Scotland. Although there were attempts by Slovak nationalists to create an ethno-linguistic division, the two different identities came from different historical experiences caused by a combination of economic and social development and their separation into different provinces of the Austro-Hungarian Empire prior to 1918. This experience meant that the new states embodied the two dominant expressions of contemporary nationalism:

- **Ethnic nationalism**: a national identity coming from a shared ethnic (or racial) heritage. This is usually identified with the principles of a common linguistic heritage and a common historical experience and often sets one national group in confrontation with another — for example, Serb versus Croat versus Bosnian Muslim; Hungarians versus Romanians or Slovaks; Albanians versus Serbs or Macedonians.
- **Civil nationalism**: a national identity coming from shared values as to how society ought to be constituted. These usually comprise a commitment to qualities such as tolerance, democracy, civil and human rights — a society as a community where citizens have an obligation to each other that goes beyond kinship and ethnicity.

Václav Havel (b. 1936), a dissident writer under the Stalinist regime in Czechoslovakia and from 1989 to 2003 president of both post-Communist Czechoslovakia and the Czech Republic, was prominent in promoting these principles. They have been embraced by the Scottish National Party as a definition of what is meant by Scottish nationalism.

What is a nation?

Many criteria have been used to establish whether or not particular groups of people qualify to be described as a nation.

Criteria most frequently used are various forms of culture — language, religion, tradition and community. Language has proved to be the most popular of these, for two reasons. First, it is one of the easiest to identify and so to use as a classification. Second, language has long been identified as a key element of nationhood — an authentic nation will possess its own language. Politics in the Austro-Hungarian Empire before 1914 was dominated by language-based nationalism. A core aspect of Israeli nationalism has been the promotion of Hebrew at the expense of the languages of European Jews — Yiddish and Ladino.

Some nationalisms have attempted to use religion as an organising principle. Israel and Pakistan (and later Bangladesh after it separated from Pakistan in 1971) are the most obvious examples. The UK has also experienced this in Northern Ireland with Protestantism (Ulster Unionism) and Catholicism (Republicanism) being employed to create two 'traditions' — nationalisms using another name.

Theses examples demonstrate how the aspiration to form a state is a central feature of modern nationalism. US President Woodrow Wilson's '14 Points' of 1918, which informed the deliberations of the Paris Peace Conference of 1919–20, created the dominant view that nations ought to have their own state. The nation was established as the 'superior' form of political community; without a state a nation would be unfulfilled and accorded only a subordinate status.

This debate revealed the distinction between state and nation. The 'nation=state' concept was counterposed to the dynastic 'multinational' empires that had collapsed in 1917–18 (Russia, Germany, Austria-Hungary and Ottoman Turkey). The nation-state concept denies the legitimacy of the 'multinational' state, whose status concealed the domination of one or two nationalities over the rest.

The multinational empires were also criticised by the racial form of nationalism. In Imperial Germany and Austria-Hungary *Volkisch* German nationalism promoted an ethnic union of the German peoples of both empires at the expense of the non-German populations of both. After the disaster of the First World War this idea evolved into Nazism. Similar 'ethnic' nationalism grew in late twentieth-century Europe. In Western Europe ethnic nationalism was primarily hostile to non-European immigration — such as the British National Party (BNP) in the UK, *Front National* in France, and the *Nationaldemokratische Partei Deutschlands* (NPD) in Germany. In Eastern Europe the targets were primarily the Roma people or national minorities within particular borders — such as Hungarians in Romania.

The distinction between race and nation can be demonstrated by examples of non-dynastic multinational states which have, nonetheless, a clear national identity. The most obvious case is the USA. Despite frequent attempts by some sections of the population to define 'Americanism' in white, Anglo-Saxon Protestant terms, the principle of the motto of the republic *E Pluribus Unum* (from many shall come one) has more or less prevailed.

Switzerland is another example of a multinational (and multi-lingual) state. Despite differences between the different sections of the population there is a distinct 'Swissness' about them that marks them apart from their linguistic neighbours in France, Germany and Italy. This 'Swissness' derives from the common political experience of self-governing communities which federated together to repel the attempts of neighbouring monarchies to absorb them. The resulting political community has over-ridden the competing claims of linguistic and ethnic nationalism.

The discussion above demonstrates that there is no single definition of a nation. Ultimately it often comes down to a psychological factor — if a group of people possess a common consciousness that they are a nation, it is almost impossible to convince them that they are not and they will act as if they are.

Liberal nationalism

This was a creation of the Enlightenment. It arose from a parallel being drawn between individuals and nations: just as individuals have the right to personal autonomy, so do nations. Every right that is attached to individuals is mirrored by one that attaches to nations. No nation can be restrained unless it threatens the autonomy of others. No nation can be restrained from making whatever choices for itself that it desires, even if outsiders consider these to be imperfect or unwise. Thus nations have the right to decide their own form of government and their own domestic policies.

As moral entities possessing these rights, nations also possess the right to self-determination and to create their own states. Ever since Woodrow Wilson this has been seen as the essential pre-requisite for self-realisation on a national scale. No nation can be itself if it does not possess its own state. In the nineteenth century attempts to form national states (such as in Greece and Italy) were great 'liberal causes'. In these cases it was argued that only national sovereignty would liberate these nations from foreign oppression.

Behind this 'Wilsonian ideal' lay the idea that the *only* legitimate basis for a state was nationality. The '14 Points' were the culmination of a struggle that liberalism had waged against dynastic states since the French Revolution. The principle had been advancing since Napoleon (1769–1821) had to style himself 'Emperor of the French' in 1804 to distinguish himself from the Bourbon 'Kings of France'.

After the collapse of the dynastic empires at the end of the First World War there was an attempt to create a structure of independent nation-states in Europe and, implicitly, in the Middle East. This trend became more powerful after 1945. The UN was created on the basis of the ideals of liberal nationalism.

First, as with individuals, the society of nations would be harmonious. This was because all nations had a similar interest in prosperity and material, scientific and cultural progress. These aims were to be mediated between international agencies such as the International Monetary Fund (IMF). Second, if dysfunctional behaviour was exhibited by one state taking aggressive action against another the UN would intervene to prevent this through the Security Council. This council would act in accordance with the UN's own constitution, the Charter. In this way the liberal order of a 'family of nations' would be preserved.

There are some liberal objections to this concept of a world of sovereign nation-states. These have become more prominent since events of the mid-1990s. The UN was regarded as totally ineffective in preventing the Rwandan genocide of 1994. UN intervention with 'peacekeeping' forces also proved to be ineffective in preventing mass murder and 'ethnic cleansing' in the Bosnian civil war in Europe (1992–95).

Both the African and European 'ethnic cleansing' were used to mount an argument that universal principles of human rights were under threat not from foreign invaders but from the rulers of the national states themselves. In these circumstances the sovereign rights of states should be over-ridden by the international community in the name of protecting human rights. This argument was forcefully made by the New Labour government of the UK in promoting intervention in the Kosovo region of Serbia in 1999 and in the civil war in Sierra Leone in 1998–99. It was given its most explicit expression in Tony Blair's 'Chicago Speech' in 1999.

This principle was invoked to legitimise the intervention of the USA, UK (and later NATO) in Afghanistan after 2001 and the invasion of Iraq in 2003. It continues to enjoy considerable support and threatens the ideological foundations of the post-1945 international order.

Conservative nationalism

This evolved after the failed liberal revolutions in Europe in 1848–49. Astute conservative politicians such as Otto von Bismarck (1815–98) in Prussia realised that nationalism could be turned into a tool to support the existing social order.

In ideological terms conservative nationalism transfers core conservative concepts from society to the nation. Identification with the nation — patriotism — is a key element of social order and stability. It provides the emotional and psychological security that conservatives hold to be so crucial to prevent social collapse. The most obvious manifestation of this is the importance given to the national flag by all conservative nationalists. It is the symbol around which all members of society can rally and with which they all identify.

Conservatives apply the concepts of heritage and tradition to nationalism. Nations are communities held together by a common history and experience. The deeds of the forefathers are passed down as a narrative, which explains the history of the nation and emphasises its positive qualities and contributions to humanity. Thus British nationalism used to emphasise the wars against France and the building of the empire, but now promotes the Second World War, and especially 1940, as the most important moment in the British narrative. In this way conservative nationalism excludes any section of the population which was not part of, or that cannot identify with, such defining moments.

This demonstrates how conservative nationalism has core features of exclusiveness. On the international level it perceives nations as potentially hostile bodies. International relations ought not to be conducted on false principles of international brotherhood but on pragmatic principles of immediate national interest. There can be no permanent allies, only permanent interests. Stability can only be achieved as 'balance of power' between states, which by definition will have conflicting interests. Conservatives are dubious of the usefulness of international organisations, especially the security functions of the UN.

Internally, the exclusive character of conservative nationalism can lead to xenophobia. Ideologically this springs from the core concept of the organic society. Translated into terms of the nation this implies an immutable ethnic and genetic nature of a nation. Once an organism has its essential features, any addition will have the nature of an alien growth threatening the body itself. This line of thinking produced the racially-based nationalism promoted by the Conservative MP Enoch Powell after 1968. In lurid language he forecast that continued large-scale non-white immigration would produce widespread social disruption and violence, as society could neither absorb nor adapt to these alien elements. This was an extravagant but accurate expression of the conservative nationalist reaction to large-scale immigration

This attitude became a dominant feature of later twentieth-century European politics. In most European countries conservative nationalists now campaign to preserve the 'authentic nature' of their societies against immigration.

Expansionist nationalism

This combines the concepts of a unique national identity with the idea of the innate superiority of your own nation. This is accompanied by the innate inferiority of other nations. At the most basic level this exhibits itself as common prejudices — particular nationalities are stupid, cowardly or corrupt. It does not take long for such ideas to develop into racism. Nationalities are all associated with intrinsic negative or positive qualities. A nation which possesses the qualities of greatness is justified in imposing its rule over other, inferior, nations.

Typically this form of nationalism is based on a national story of greatness. Benito Mussolini (1883–1945) justified Italian expansion into Africa by reference to the Roman empire and the Renaissance. This provided the basis for a 'national mission' which legitimated the Italian idea of an African empire. Many other expansionist nationalisms have used the idea of the 'civilising mission' to justify themselves. The British and French colonial empires and the German nationalist campaign against the Slavs were all driven in part by different views of a national history that was built around the special qualities of their own nation that it was duty bound to export to other less advanced areas of the world.

From this it followed that all forms of expansionist nationalism favoured aggression and delighted in the military exploits of the nation. These forms varied between countries. In Germany there was the explicit militarism of the Prussian state and army, while in Britain the focus varied between glorification of naval heroes to celebrating the deeds of daring individuals on various parts of the imperial frontier.

Before 1914, expansionist nationalism found expression in many countries in well-funded pressure groups such as Navy and Colonial leagues. With substantial business, press and political support these campaigned for policies of imperial advance and military expansion. The widespread nature of this form of nationalism was a principal source of international tension after 1900 and many historians argue that its influence made the outbreak of war at some point almost inevitable.

One reason for the success of this form of nationalism was the widespread acceptance of 'social Darwinism'. This took the form of a crude misapplication of the principle of natural selection to international relations. It legitimised war as the playing out of an integral process — the victory of 'fitter' nations over the 'unfit'.

It is clear how these ideas grew into the expansionist nationalism that is associated with fascism. Fascism did not only draw on existing theories of national greatness and myths of the national mission. All forms of fascism absorbed social Darwinism and raised it to unprecedented levels. Not only were other inferior nations there to be conquered, they could also be eliminated from the face of the earth. Here the nation became the only identity which possessed any reality — what the French conservative nationalist turned fascist Charles Maurras (1868–1952) called 'integral nationalism'. The necessary consequence of individuals becoming absorbed into their own national community was that they only saw national stereotypes in others — to be admired, despised, conquered or eliminated.

Anti-colonial nationalism

In many ways this is the mirror-image of expansionist nationalism. Here nationalism becomes the means for the liberation of colonial territories. It also becomes the agent for the creation of a post-colonial political entity.

The first examples of anti-colonial nationalism consciously modelled themselves on the prime example of liberal nationalism. Both the Irish Nationalist Movement and the early Indian National Congress took the Italian national movement of the 1820s to 1860s as their model. Both aimed to create a unified nation on the liberal principles that they imagined the Italian nationalists Guiseppe Mazzini (1805–72) and Guiseppe Garibaldi (1807–82) had fought for. Many early Indian nationalists were great admirers of Britain. They wished to embrace all aspects of 'Britishness', including parliamentary democracy. Many of the nationalist movements in other British colonies began with similar objectives. Their nationalism attacked Britain for ruling in an 'un-British' fashion.

These ideas moved into a critique of imperial rule. Imperial rule 'drained' the colonies of their wealth and resources, using them as a source of cheap raw materials and labour. Economic development was further retarded by the use of the colonies as a secure market for the home country's manufactured goods. Since local industries would be competitors, the imperial government restricted and suppressed their development. Nationalism thus became seen as the only means for social change and economic progress. It was associated with strategies for indigenous economic development and national self-sufficiency.

Such policies were pursued in many African countries after independence. By the 1960s the success of the Communist party in China and Vietnam provided another model for post-colonial nationalism. This was the road of 'national liberation', followed wherever the colonial powers did not de-colonise, as in the Portuguese African empire or in the white-settled states of Rhodesia and South Africa. After the victory of the Cuban revolution in 1959 it was applied to South American countries ruled by pro-American aristocratic elites. National liberation implied an armed struggle against the rulers, but one waged by the poorest in society. The struggles would not only eject the rulers but would also transform society after their victory. The Cuban revolution was seen as a particularly attractive model. It was credited with defeating endemic racism, and bringing universal welfare, education and healthcare to the impoverished majority of a previously deeply divided society.

With the collapse of colonialism in Africa, nationalism in former colonies moved into a 'post-colonial' phase. This had features that varied across the world. In the Middle East it has taken a predominantly anti-Western form linked to the central issue of Israel–Palestine. As secular nationalist regimes lost their legitimacy after successive failures to resolve the fate of the Palestinians, or to secure economic prosperity for their populations, they were challenged by assertive Islamicist forces.

This tendency first emerged during the Iranian revolution of 1979, but is now present across the Muslim world. These ideas combine anti-Western attitudes with social conservatism. In South America anti-Americanism is still a major element in nationalist ideas, as shown by the government of President Chávez who came to power in 1999 in Venezuela and other 'indigenous' nationalist movements in Ecuador, Peru and Bolivia. They glorify the pre-Columban indigenous cultures at the expense of the 'European' Spanish dominated culture created by colonial rule and continued by the elites who ruled the countries after independence from Spain.

Feminism

Although the contemporary sense in which the ideology of feminism is understood has only been in general use since the 1960s, as a general ideology it has been in existence since the era of the French Revolution. It is based on two interrelated propositions: that women are discriminated against because they *are* women; and that this discrimination should be challenged and removed. Beyond this, there is a wide diversity of views and objectives within the feminist movement. Some of these are feminist versions of other ideologies, such as liberalism and socialism. Some, such as radical feminism, are rejections of all existing 'male' ideologies.

Feminists have always believed that social change is needed to achieve full rights for women. As such, feminist movements have included demands for specific and immediate reforms with their more long-term general objectives. This has led to the characterisation of feminist movements as taking place within specific 'waves'. First-wave feminism relates to nineteenth-century campaigns for legal autonomy, the right to enter professions and crucially the right to vote. This 'wave' is usually said to have ended with the gaining of the suffrage for women, in most industrialised states, around 1918–20. Second-wave feminism relates to the era from the 1960s onwards, which produced the modern Women's Movement. Here there were again issues of legal equality, such as equal pay and equal access to employment. Under the influence of the American feminist Betty Friedan (1921–2006) there was central attention to issues of consciousness. She attacked cultural and ideological pressures that encouraged women to define themselves primarily in feminine and domestic terms. Later feminist writers such as Kate Millett (b. 1934), Germaine Greer (b. 1939) and Eva Figes (b. 1932) wrote about the nature of the female condition, about the social conditioning that drove women to accommodate themselves to the demands of male-dominated society. The process of the domination of women by men was given a new term — 'sexism'.

The result of these concerns was to open up the family as a central arena of political analysis and campaigning. This produced another central feature of second-wave feminism — the concept of the 'public' and private' spheres of life. Whereas the first wave had concentrated almost exclusively on public areas — the law, politics and the professions — the second wave argued that the key location of women's oppression was within the family. Only by addressing this could women truly be liberated to fulfil their personalities. This was the origin of the distinctive slogan of the Women's Movement: 'the personal is political'.

Although the Women's Movement itself fragmented in most Western countries at the end of the 1970s, usually over issues connected with how to organise and campaign, by the 1990s many people were arguing that its concerns had been absorbed into mainstream political discourse. The central feminist concept of gender is now incorporated into much of public policy and academic discussion.

Many feminists now argue that there has in fact been an ideological retreat. New generations of women are largely unaware of the nature of their condition, and sexist attitudes are recovering in the forms of 'laddish' and celebrity culture. Women are once again viewing themselves in terms of their attractiveness to men and seeing freedom in terms of the adoption of some of the most objectionable aspects of male behaviour, such as the large-scale consumption of alcohol known as 'binge drinking'. This is combined with a renewed idealisation of marriage and childbirth as the ideal for women, again promoted through the medium of popular celebrity culture and its associated media. For feminists this 'post-feminism' is a reactionary process, and urgently needs to be countered by a recapturing of the ideals and campaigning spirit of the 1960s and 1970s.

Sex and gender

These refer to the crucial distinctions between men and women. The term *sex* is used to describe the biological divide between individuals and, most importantly, the different roles played in the procreation and delivery of children which arise from the specific, unavoidable, sexual features of men and women. Feminists term these roles 'biological' destiny, but do not accept them as having inevitable social consequences.

Feminists argue that *gender*, that is the roles that women and men adopt in society, is not predestined or necessarily linked with biological roles of sex. This is where all feminists disagree with conservatives, who argue that these roles are natural, and cannot be altered without destabilising the foundations of society. Feminists say that gender roles are determined by culture, that they are therefore not permanent, and changing them will improve the condition of society. They point out that there is no absolute uniform way to raise children and that it is technically easy to alter the structure of domestic life. The notion that the 'nuclear family' of two generations in one unit is traditional has been undermined by historical studies demonstrating that various forms of extended family units were commonplace in different parts of (for instance) Britain in the recent past.

Gender extends beyond immediate family and domestic arrangements. It applies to the ways in which women and men are seen in the context of society and includes the whole range of gender roles including those ascribed to men and women in terms of stereotypes. At one level this includes the idea of men's jobs and women's jobs. Traditionally, heavy manual occupations such as construction and engineering have been viewed as 'male', while those tasks requiring manual dexterity such as sewing, typing or giving physical care such as nursing have been categorised as 'women's work'.

These perceptions of gender differences were used in the past to argue for the exclusion of women from the vote, and are still used today to explain the existence of the 'glass ceiling', the phenomenon whereby few women are promoted to very senior positions in organisations, despite there being no formal prohibition to such promotion. The glass ceiling theory holds that there is inherent organisational bias that women are not suited to these posts. This argument often takes the form that women are not as whole-heartedly committed to the organisation as their male colleagues. This is a contemporary reflection of gender roles in that it implies that women have a commitment to family and children that is greater than that of men and this precludes total commitment to their employment.

Feminists argue that the glass ceiling is the contemporary expression of the 'public–private' divide. This concept is used by feminists to explain how women can be systematically excluded from public and social affairs: to keep them at home (in the private sphere) an ideological justification has been created that women are the rulers of this private realm. 'Male dominated' ideologies ascribe equal value to the two realms (women as being the 'power behind the throne'). Feminists argue that this is a manoeuvre to legitimise the permanent exclusion of women from political power and their ability to participate in all forms of professional employment possessing significant public influence and economic power.

Patriarchy

This concept is a unique feature of feminism. It is also an issue that can seriously divide feminists; different strands of feminism ascribe very different levels of importance to it. While socialist feminists tend to view patriarchy as a subsidiary feature of their interpretation of male oppression, or may totally reject the idea, most radical feminists place it at the centre of their world view. Liberal feminists take an ambivalent approach, tending to apply the influence of patriarchy only to the 'public sphere'.

Literally, the term patriarchy means 'rule of the father'. Most feminists interpret it as meaning the rule of men over society as a whole. Some argue that it is the rule of the male head of the family over everyone else, including 'junior' males. According to this view the patriarchal family becomes the means by which all members of society are socialised into an acceptance of the male domination of the public sphere of life. Thus some feminists see patriarchy as the foundation of a multi-layered social conservatism, both in gender and generational terms.

The radical view

Radical feminists such as Kate Millett view patriarchy as being the core of all social and political relations. It serves as a sexual division of labour and a means of organising society founded on biology rather than history or economics.

All men, no matter what their social status or ethnicity, are bound together at the top of a hierarchy which creates a bond of solidarity between them. All men wish to use this power to control 'their' women, be it in how they spend their time, their careers, or who they may marry. It is a universal form of the oppression of women, by which means male-dominated society constantly reproduces itself.

The liberal view

For liberal feminists, the concern over the patriarchal system is the way in which it influences the public sphere of life. They are concerned with its application in the fields of politics, employment and the economy. They point to male domination of senior positions in politics, the professions and in business, resulting in policy-making that reflects male priorities. This has made it difficult for women to set their own priorities in public life and work, notably in incorporating opportunities to raise a family without sacrificing their career path. The glass ceiling is an example of the pervasive presence of patriarchy within society, which needs to be broken by a combination of legislation and public policy. To support their strategy of gradual reforms liberal feminists point to progress made since 1997 in legislation on paternity and maternity leave, the fact that Parliament has been organised along more accommodating lines for the parents of young children, and the pressure which has resulted in the major parties promoting the selection of more women as parliamentary candidates. The fact that there has been progress is used as an example of how it is possible to make changes; the often very slow rate of change is used to demonstrate how deep-rooted patriarchal attitudes are in society.

The socialist view

Socialist feminists have incorporated patriarchy into a theory of 'double oppression'. Working-class women are oppressed both at work by their employers and at home by the patriarchal family. Despite working, and in many cases bringing in the principal family income, women still have to assume the domestic roles of homemaker and primary carer of children. This situation is linked with the concept of 'unpaid labour'. Socialist feminists see capitalism as being subsidised by women who raise its future workforce free of charge. Women also maintain the present workforce free of charge by their unpaid labour in the home. As a result, some socialist feminist groups have organised campaigns for 'wages for housework'.

In general, socialist feminists see the solution of women's oppression as being the overthrow of capitalism. They regard patriarchy, as with all oppression suffered by women, as ultimately created by class oppression. This leads some socialist feminists to relegate patriarchy to the position of a mere symptom of women's oppression, rather than its fundamental cause as argued by radical feminists.

Liberal feminism

This was the original form of feminism, put forward by early feminists such as Mary Wollestonecraft (1759–97) who were products of the Enlightenment and shared the same assumptions about human rationality as the founders of liberalism. Wollestonecraft's book *A Vindication of the Rights of Women* (1792) was a reflection of Tom Paine's book *The Rights of Man* (1791). Her arguments for women's human rights and rights to education thus had their roots in liberal thought.

This first-wave feminism generated the movements for political enfranchisement in the USA (led by figures such as Elizabeth Cady Stanton, 1815–1902) and in the UK (led by figures such as Millicent Garrett Fawcett, 1847–1929 and Emmeline Pankhurst, 1858–1928). These were paralleled by attempts to open up the professions to women, including medicine, where Elizabeth Garrett Anderson (1836–1917) was a pioneer. The arguments were based on the liberal grounds that women are rational beings who were being denied their natural rights by gender discrimination.

By 1920 these campaigns had been at least formally won. Women had the vote in most industrialised countries and most professions were open to them, at least in name.

The wider, informal, gender-based discrimination practised across society generated second-wave feminism in the 1960s. A decisive moment came with the publication of Betty Friedan's book *The Feminine Mystique* in 1963. She argued that the 'mystique' was the informal cultural myth that women seek 'femininity' and 'domestic bliss'. This was particularly strong in the USA, where women were constantly portrayed as playing out the roles of mother and homemaker. This stereotype was seen by feminists as a celebration of women's confinement to the private sphere. Friedan argued that this mystique was psychologically oppressive of women, as they were unable to achieve the fundamental liberal objective of personal self-realisation.

Second-wave feminism led to a series of campaigns for equal rights in the USA and other industrialised countries. One main objective was equal pay for equal work, which was eventually gained in the UK by the passing of the Equal Pay Act (1970). The campaigns succeeded in gaining a series of pieces of equal rights gains in anti-discrimination legislation in many countries, notably in the European Union.

Liberal feminists applaud the way in which women have been able to advance to high political office and to the top of many professions and business management. They also point to the emergence of powerful women in different sections of the entertainment industry as examples of the progress that has been made, emphasising that this should be celebrated and emulated more generally across society.

In non-industrialised countries liberal feminists continue to highlight the lack of more basic rights for women. In many countries women still do not possess formal legal equality. Patriarchal attitudes are often entrenched in law, especially in regard to family affairs. Liberal feminists bitterly oppose Islamic movements, on the grounds that they attempt to reintroduce or reinforce ultra-conservative forms of patriarchal oppression, for instance as in the provisions of Sharia law. More widely, liberal feminists argue that women are denied fundamental rights such as access to education and basic healthcare, and are the victims of systematic sexual violence in many civil wars. These concerns have sometimes led feminists in African, Asian and South American countries to accuse Western liberal feminists of reflecting the concerns of white middle-class professionals in industrialised countries to the exclusion of all other women.

There is also a 'neo-liberal' version of liberal feminism. This supports positive discrimination for women in employment because discrimination against women is seen as distorting the labour market by preventing the most effective allocation of human resources.

Socialist feminism

Many early socialists were supporters of first-wave feminism. Emmeline Pankhurst, founder of the Women's Social and Political union — the Suffragettes — began her political career as a leading member of the Independent Labour Party (ILP) in Manchester. Her campaign always enjoyed the support of many leading ILP members, notably Keir Hardie, first ILP MP and leader of the Labour Party before 1914. Socialist groups such as the Fabian Society devoted much time and effort to discussing the 'Woman Question', especially over issues of employment and social legislation.

The first major socialist theoretical contribution to feminist issues came with Frederick Engels' book *The Origins of the Family, Private Property and the State* (1884). As the title suggests, Engels argued that women's oppression arose out of the creation of class society. In particular, capitalism abolished most forms of property ownership by women, and most remaining forms of inheritance in the female line. The principle of property ownership was extended into the family of the ruling class itself. Men were assigned property rights over the female and non-adult members of the family. This created the model of the 'bourgeois family', which was then imposed on other classes in society. It had to be imposed on the working class, since by definition they did not possess private property.

More recent socialist feminists such as Sheila Rowbotham (b. 1943) have argued that women suffer from the 'double oppression' of being workers and mothers and homemakers. From this they argue that women constitute a reserve army of labour for capitalism. In this theory women are seen as a predominantly low-skilled pool of labour which is recruited to the labour force in times of expansion and then laid off in recession. They also argue that in their role as mothers and homemakers, women are the producers of the new labour force and the maintenance staff for existing workers.

Socialist feminists have expressed a wide range of views. Orthodox Communists of the Stalinist tradition tended to see women's oppression simply as a by-product of capitalism that would dissolve once capitalism was overthrown. More commonly, other Marxists have argued for specific strategies to combat women's oppression from a class perspective. These entail rejecting the idea that there is any common ground with women from the ruling class and insisting that working-class women have funda-mental common interests with male members of the working class. This last point has at times created severe tensions within socialist groups. Women who accept the validity of some form of patriarchy theory have frequently made the issue of separate organisations for women within wider socialist groups a major point of contention. They have often been criticised for promoting strategies that will divide the working class and weaken the struggle against capitalism.

Since the mid-1990s the success of a neo-revisionist socialism of the Third Way type has had a significant impact on socialist feminists who support social democratic parties. The general movement of the Third Way towards the principles of modern liberalism has led to an embracing of goals more usually associated with liberal feminism. Such socialist feminists emphasise legal gains over employment rights and placing pressure on political, professional and business organisations to promote women. Success is often measured by the number of senior managers and execu-tives in high-profile positions. Socialist feminists outside the influence of social democratic parties do not accept this 'equality of opportunity' measure, looking instead at the position of women at the lowest level of businesses and organisations — an 'equality of outcome' measure.

Radical feminism

This tendency arose out of debates within the Women's Movement in the early 1970s. The Women's Movement was the loose association of campaigning and self-education groups created by the second-wave feminism of the 1960s. Arguments about patriarchy and relations with men propelled many women towards political separatism — an insistence on women-only organisations. This extended into arguing for the complete exclusion of men from campaigns on women's issues, even as supporters on demonstrations organised in support of women's issues. Radical feminism can therefore be defined as an ideology of separatism.

Many radical feminists took inspiration from the writings of the French philosopher Simone de Beauvoir (1909–86), especially her book *The Second Sex* (1949). She argued that gender dominates women's lives. The stereotypical 'male' image is portrayed as the desirable social norm, with the implication that the 'female' is therefore a deviation. Following this other writers such as Eva Figes and Germaine Greer dealt with the imposition of male-created stereotypes of femininity on women. Greer, in *The Female Eunuch* (1970) argued that women are socialised into totally passive sexual roles. Other writers such as Susan Brownmiller in her book *Against Our Will* (1975) took the position that male control of women through violence and abuse is central to the success of patriarchy.

In this way radical feminists came to argue for separation on the basis that gender was the primary social and political division within society. As a consequence they pioneered the slogan that 'the personal is political', which first appeared in 1970, thus rejecting the liberal feminist argument that the public and private spheres are distinct. Radical feminists insisted that the most important political contests are fought out between men and women in their own personal relations and that this political control operated everywhere, in all classes and in all societies. The task was to encourage all women to become 'women-centered' and to turn away from class, ethnic or religious identities. Sisterhood was the objective, as it was the only means to liberation for women, and women's consciousness had to be raised to achieve this.

Some radical feminists moved further into separatist campaigning such as 'political lesbianism'. This was intended to be a cultural rather than a sexual strategy. Lesbianism was portrayed as the ultimate rejection of patriarchal society, in the choice of a completely 'women-centered' world; since sexual oppression was *the* prime organising factor of society, the best way to undermine patriarchy was to reject sexual relations with men completely. From this perspective, contemporary radical feminists such as Sheila Jeffreys (b. 1948) are dismayed by 'post-feminist' women who appear to embrace marriage and childbearing as liberating and fulfilling experiences. To Jeffreys they appear to be volunteering to reverse any progress that has been made towards women's liberation. They are embracing the core features of their own oppression and willingly celebrating fundamental features of sexual stereotyping as portrayed through women's magazines and celebrity culture.

Anti-feminism

Fundamentally, this is the conservative critique of all kinds of feminist thought. In general the ideas of anti-feminism follow the central principles of conservatism, although as we have seen neo-liberals embrace a specific version of liberal feminist ideas. While some anti-feminism derives from roles ascribed to women in the texts of revealed religion, most criticisms come from a view of society.

One attack derives from the core conservative concept of the 'organic society'. Since this argues that every established social feature serves a fundamental function in society, then it follows that sexual divisions of labour and social roles are destiny. Women, by means of their emotional and psychological features, as well as their physical natures, are naturally fitted for the roles of mother and homemaker. Attempts to move women away from this model will, in general, be socially dysfunctional, provoking an increased incidence of family breakdown. Children will be ineffectively parented and socialised, which in turn will lead to increased levels of anti-social behaviour. These arguments lead to opposition to government policies aimed at increasing women's participation in work. Instead many conservatives say that more support should be given to married couples through the tax system and that mothers should be encouraged to remain at home with young children.

An associated point is that the patriarchal family has been vindicated by history — it has 'stood the test of time'. This argument takes on a universalist aura as its proponents often go on to argue that the patriarchal family has existed over long periods of time and in a wide range of societies. The family is the natural unit of society and women's role within it is so fundamental to its survival that any attempt to alter the structure must produce extreme negative results that will destabilise society as a whole.

Attempts are made to deal with feminist charges of the oppression of women by employing the 'different but equal' response, that fixed roles should not imply any notions of superiority or inferiority. Both male and female roles are essential for the effective functioning of society, and so are due equal respect. This position often concedes that equal respect is not always given to women, and that an element of 're-education' of some men is necessary to address the problem. Such conservatives criticise abusive and patronising language directed at women and the lack of public recognition of their contributions to society.

Ecologism

Although the term 'ecology' has existed since 1866 (it was created by the German zoologist Ernst Hoeckel), it has only developed as a coherent ideology with a significant following since the 1960s. Ecology is now associated with the wide-ranging environmentalist movement and the 'green' political parties which have emerged from it. Its primary concern is the preservation of the ecosystems — the self-regulating natural systems — that make up life on Earth.

As an ideology that deals with the relations between living organisms (especially humans) and their environment, ecology has a number of strands. Some of these have their origins in nineteenth-century thought. One example is pastoralism, or the idealisation of rural life, in contrast to that of the city. Pastoralism was associated with a distaste for both the nature and the effects of industrialisation. It led to a variety of entirely disparate consequences, such as the rural romanticism of the novels of J. R. R. Tolkien to the 1920s German back-to-nature youth movement, the *Wandervogel*. This latter was appropriated by the Nazis and absorbed into their myths of the peasantry as the carrier of the essential nature of the German *volk*.

These examples demonstrate how ecologism can range widely across the existing ideological spectrum. There are eco-socialists, eco-feminists, conservative ecologists and the pastoralist wings of ultra-conservative and fascist movements in Europe and the USA. All begin from the presumption that there is a crisis in the relationship between humans and the environment. Some go as far as to say that this crisis threatens the planet itself.

Since the 1970s there has been growing international recognition by governments and multinational agencies that there are urgent environmental issues requiring international action. Treaties have been concluded that are aimed at preserving the ozone layer through banning the use of CFCs, and also addressing climate change, such as the Kyoto Protocols. There has been a proliferation of insider (such as the Worldwide Fund for Nature — WWF) and outsider (anti-road and airport campaigners) pressure groups addressing these issues. In the twenty-first century, environmental concerns have proved to be the type of issue for which large numbers of young people are most easily mobilised into political activity.

The prospect is that the influence, and thus the importance, of ecological ideologies can only grow over the next decade

Ecology

This topic relates to the core concepts of the ideology. Ecologists hold that the single most important aspect of human existence is its relationship with the natural world — 'the planet Earth'. Every other distinction, class, nation, race, gender and religion, is subordinate to this, because they are all determined by it.

Ecologists tend to accuse supporters of other ideologies of various degrees of anthropocentrism. This means the placing of humanity at the centre of all existence and of assuming that the rest of the world — all living things and all mineral resources — simply exist for the benefit of humanity. The consequence of this anthropocentric belief is the unrestrained exploitation of natural resources for short-term economic advantage. Prime examples of such exploitation are the destruction of large parts of the Amazon rainforest for cattle and soya production, and industrialised fishing techniques, which have exhausted many fish stocks around the world. Both practices destroy ecosystems, with global impact, but are justified on the grounds of economic development. This is why many ecologists accuse other ideological traditions of merely being different forms of 'industrialism', since they all support some form of economic expansion.

Ecologists argue that nature and ecosystems must be the starting point of human concern. Policies must be aimed at the preservation of nature and the complex inter-related ecosystems that allow the world to function. This is why they now place over-riding importance on addressing climate change and the need to reduce human-produced carbon emissions. Ecologists see human-created climate change as the definitive proof of their arguments and the ultimate justification for the changes in political, social and economic behaviour that their ideology demands.

However, ecologists differ deeply on how to achieve these objectives. In this they in some ways mirror differences found in other ideological traditions. 'Shallow' ecology might usefully be seen as ecological reformism. Its supporters place human needs at the centre of political concern, but agree that human survival requires a series of major changes in how humans approach their environment. They therefore support measures to limit over-fishing and forest destruction, and promote government measures to reduce the levels of carbon emissions on a global scale. They employ terms such as 'sustainable development' and 'conservation'. Some shallow ecologists also argue for population control on the basis that fewer humans will place fewer demands on the resources of the planet.

The Norwegian philosopher Arne Naess (1912–2009), who coined the term shallow ecology, was himself a proponent of its mirror image — 'deep ecology'. This is an ideology of eco-centrism, the view that the natural world must have primary impor-tance in political concerns. Deep ecologists dispute the primacy of human needs and concerns, and many reject any notion that humans are in any way superior to other life forms (in this sense, animal rights campaigners are deep ecologists). They demand a fundamental retreat from contemporary industrial society, from globalisation and from the increased consumption of material goods. Implicitly at least, they also demand a substantial reduction in the size of the human population. For this they have faced a range of criticisms from other ecologists, including mysticism and irrationality. Many followers of other ideologies see deep ecology as a fundamental ideological assault on the entire basis of the Enlightenment (that it is possible to know the world in all its aspects and for human action to be able to decide the course of events).

These criticisms refer to elements within deep ecology that embrace religious and mystical beliefs associated with Asian, African and South American religions. The notion of holism — that all beings are simply aspects of one unified creation — are common to many of these. Since such a concept is beyond evidential proof or disproof (at least at present) then by definition it is a myth. The concept of holism was given a contemporary form in the 'Gaia' theory of the Canadian scientist James Lovelock. Gaia theory conceives of the Earth as a single living ecosystem, which is self-regulating. This implies that dysfunctional behaviour by humans will only result in their displacement by Gaia. However, Lovelock himself displays shallow ecological tendencies in his support for the widespread development of nuclear power as a solution to global warming.

Sustainability

Ecologists use this concept to criticise the dominant concern of most other ideologies to expand industrial output indefinitely: 'industrialism'. Their argument rests on the idea that all resources on the planet are finite. Any economic activity that assumes there will be an unending supply of raw materials is doomed to failure. Worse than failure, the attempt will despoil and exhaust the Earth's resources.

Metaphors have been used to encapsulate this concept, notably that of 'spaceship Earth'. Here the Earth is a limited vessel whose resources will eventually be used up. Raw materials are part of this closed system and they will be used up, probably relatively soon. Fossil fuels such as oil cannot be replaced. This idea lies behind the concept of 'peak oil' — that the maximum levels of petroleum production have already been passed. From now on the extraction rates of oil are and will exceed the rate of new discoveries. Moreover any new discoveries or exploitations of existing fields are increasingly expensive and damaging to the environment, such as those in the Arctic. If the global economy continues its dependence on oil, then decay and decline will be the result.

Ernst Shumacher (1911–77) argued that the root of the problem lies in the government and business practice of regarding raw materials as a flow of income (constantly refreshed) rather than a stock of capital (being constantly depleted). Others have highlighted the despoliation of natural resources such as common land (now under threat of total elimination in industrialised states) and the sea, which is now being colonised by states and businesses. States are now claiming control of ever greater economic zones away from their coasts, while fishing businesses are ruthlessly exploiting stocks across the globe as if they were wild fruit for the picking. Competitive extraction interests see no further than the short-term benefits to individual businesses, and so do not care what the effects on the natural environment are. This is called 'the tragedy of the commons'. In contrast, community control of these land and marine resources means that they will be maintained and nurtured.

A number of remedies are being proposed to meet the problem of sustainability. 'Light' greens (another term for shallow ecologists) advocate the use of approaches which involve action by states. Such actions include the management of fishing stocks through the introduction of fishing bans and quotas such as those imposed by the European Union. This strategy faces problems where there are weak states, such as in Africa, facing powerful enterprises based in industrialised countries. These businesses often obtain permission to carry out stock-exhausting fishing by offering short-term, very modest economic 'concessions' to the governments concerned. Other examples of state action are contained in the initial economic proposals of the Obama administration in the USA. These aim to wean the USA away from its dependence on oil by promoting renewable power sources such as solar energy and wind power. Such an approach still implies the objective of increasing production and material prosperity but transforms the ways in which they are to be achieved.

'Dark' greens (deep ecologists) regard such strategies as dangerously naïve. They are either impossible to achieve, given the current influence of large enterprises and their state agency allies, or will take so long to achieve that the 'tipping point' for systemic breakdown will have been passed long before they have any effect. Dark greens argue that the only effective response to the crisis of the Earth is fundamentally to change global attitudes to material wealth and economic growth. Both will have to be drastically scaled back to a level of 'zero growth', and accompanied by a reduction in the global population. This reduced population will have to be much more self-sufficient, with no core reliance on imported goods. The consequences of this would be very limited international trade and movement of people.

Environmental ethics

These centre around the ecological critique of the anthropocentric concerns of other ideologies and philosophies. For ecologists, humanity is not the be all and end all of existence, and the rest of existence is not here simply to service humanity. Moreover, humans are not free just to think of themselves. They have an obligation to consider the impact of their actions on generations yet unborn, going far beyond those who will be born to anyone alive at this moment.

Some existing ideologies do have something to say on this point. Conservative thought, with its emphasis on tradition and the importance of inheritance following the ideas of Edmund Burke (1729–97), easily absorbs the idea of 'conserving' for generations yet unborn. Socialism, with its emphasis on collaboration and sociability, implies concern for society as an unending phenomenon. Ecologists are set apart from these ideologies by their emphasis on concern for the future best interests of the natural world.

The Australian philosopher Peter Singer (b. 1946) has had a profound impact on environmental ethics. His arguments that animals have moral rights (because they can suffer pain and fear) have had a significant impact on the animal rights movement. His propositions have been extended (far beyond what he would himself support) to support pressure group campaigns against animal testing in scientific establishments and the industrial production of animals for the fur trade. For campaigners, ethics *demand* that action be taken against them; indifference is to be complicit in a criminal activity.

Beyond this limited, but high-profile, tendency, ecologists have other ethical concerns. They place nature at the centre of existence, while artificial processes are perceived as possessing limited intrinsic value. Thus the engineering of landscapes should be avoided, as it imposes human designs on natural features that have as much right to be there as we do. Ideally as much land as possible should be allowed to revert to wilderness. This is the idea of bio-centric equality. Every living being has equal value to each other and has equal rights, and they are all part of an interdependent whole.

Ecologism holds that if humans followed ethical concerns they would feel better about themselves. They would become closer to the fulfillment of their personalities because freeing themselves from the pursuit of material wealth frees their own personalities. This line of thinking has led many ecologists towards 'New Age' ideas, based on various forms of mysticism. This aspect of environmental ethics has attracted increasing criticism for allegedly legitimising prejudice and superstition. The debate is especially bitter over 'alternative' medicines and health therapies. These treatments are criticised for lacking any evidence base and for becoming major businesses masquerading as ethical alternatives to industrialised Western medicine.

Right-wing ecology

This began with anti-industrial movements in the nineteenth century, linked with elements of the Romantic cultural movement. Right-wing ecologists idealised the image of a pre-industrial, harmonious agrarian society. This image frequently drifted into an idealisation of medieval society. Such societies had a hierarchical basis of aristocratic heroism which was profoundly reactionary in the context of industrialising nineteenth-century Europe.

In the twentieth century the Nazi movement absorbed and expanded these ideas into its 'Blood and Soil' theory. The true essence of the German nation — its *Volksgeist* — was to be found in the independent peasant family. This version of reactionary ecologism vanished with the Nazi defeat in 1945, although certain themes continue to resurface in ecological writing.

Mainstream conservative ecology has been directed towards nostalgic attempts to maintain and if possible expand remaining rural areas. This has taken the form of stressing the conservation of existing rural landscapes and opposition to urban expansion. There are frequent campaigns against developments as varied as golf courses and upland wind farms. All of these ideas, although hostile in various ways at least to the expansion of industrial society, are conservative because they look back to an ideal time (even if it is only a version of Edwardian England 1901–14). Most other forms of ecological anti-industrialism have a post- rather than a pre-industrial concept of an ideal world.

There is a neo-liberal variant of right-wing ecology. This forms around the concept of the 'green pound'. Here the market is regarded as the core factor in transforming the environment and embedding conservation aims. It looks to eco-friendly tax regimes and to market solutions on a global scale, such as carbon trading between states to resolve the issue of climate change. The green pound strategy relies on capitalist enterprises acting rationally to create sustainable development over a long time scale. The argument is that this will ensure the permanent security both of individual enterprises and of the capitalist system as a whole.

Left-wing ecology

In contrast, 'green socialism' assumes that capitalism is the prime threat to the environment. Many green parties contain large numbers of members who have previously been socialist activists. This is particularly true of the most successful of such parties, the German Green Party. For them 'industrialism' is simply capitalism, which colonises and despoils the entire globe in its drive for profits. Environmental destruction is a byproduct and symptom of capitalism's drive to subordinate everything else to its need for profits. The survival of the environment therefore demands the overthrow of capitalism. Once this has been done, production will be undertaken for need, wasteful competition and over-production will end and sustainable development will become a possibility.

To meet criticisms of the Communist states of the old Eastern Bloc, which developed industries on a scale that produced many instances of massive environmental destruction, most green socialists resort to the 'state capitalist' explanation. This is the theory that after 1929 the USSR, and the various states which followed its model of economic development, were no longer authentically Communist. Joseph Stalin presided over a counter-revolution whereby the state functioned as one giant capitalist, competing on a world scale with other capitalist states. Such states therefore behaved as did any individual capitalist enterprise, and were concerned with short-term gains rather than the long-term impact on the environment.

It is possible to see ecologism as being the home of the greater part of contemporary anarchism. Hostility to the state, to private property and to capitalism are features of most strands of anarchist thought. These fit easily with the core concerns of ecology. The anarchist vision of a society living and working in complete harmony with itself is easily seen as an authentic ecological image of post-industrial society. The anarchist aim of small self-governing communities is again one that is at the core of the ecological ideal for society. The writings of classical anarchists such as Kropotkin (1842–1921) can be used to support mainstream ecological views, as they are based on the principles of the laws of nature. However, the presence of such significant 'eco-anarchist' tendencies serves to exacerbate tensions already present between the 'realo wing' which wishes to work within existing social and governmental institutions and the 'fundis' who wish to do away with them altogether. The anarchist tradition of direct action is appealing to people in the 'fundi' wing and it is a major factor in expanding the influence of eco-anarchism.

Eco-feminism

It is a short step from radical feminist views on women's oppression to an identification of industrial society with the core features of patriarchy. The despoliation of the natural world appears as another aspect of the male subjugation of women. The term rape is used to describe both phenomena. Eco-feminism moves from the radical feminist argument that maleness is a rejection of nature to the idea that the rejection of nature by industrialism is yet another expression of maleness. Men portray themselves as the masters of nature in the same way that they do as masters of women.

These ideas fit into the radical feminist notion that women possess 'essential' characteristics that place them close to nature. They draw on contemporary expressions of the Earth-mother concept originally found in many early religions. Women's role in nurturing children provides them with this affinity to nature, and makes them the guardians of the natural world. Female cooperativeness also places them close to nature, while male competitiveness threatens to destroy nature because it does not place any intrinsic value on it. Like the rest of existence, it is simply a resource to be used by men.

Eco-feminism views culture and civilisation as being products of patriarchal society. It looks back to the natural knowledge of 'wise women', who flourished before the final victory of patriarchy with the rise of industrial society. These features tend to drive eco-feminism into a vision of pre-industrial society, the celebration of an image of a world that existed before industrialisation and capitalism. The problem for pure eco-feminism is that while it can inspire individuals who can create spaces for their lifestyles on the margins of existing societies, it suggests no agency for transforming society as a whole. In this it is different from the other major strands of ecological thought, each of which generates its own vision of the agency of change, be it the green pound, the working class, or direct action.

Multiculturalism

Cultural diversity is a central issue in political debate. The politics of contemporary Europe are dominated by bitter debates over the ways in which populations of immigrant origin can be integrated with the host populations. Parties of the far right, such as the Freedom Party in Austria, *Front National* in France, *Vlaams Belang* in Belgium and British National Party in the UK, argue that immigrant populations constitute a fundamental threat to the cultural integrity of the states in which they live. These parties argue for policies ranging from assimilation into host populations to compulsory repatriation to countries of origin.

However, multiculturalism was a key area of conflict long before the post-1945 waves of migration. Irreconcilable ethnic divisions were crucial in undermining the Austro-Hungarian Empire before 1914. They led directly to the outbreak of war in 1914 — the Austrian attack on Serbia was the ruling elite's 'solution by violence' to national disputes within the empire. The long-running civil war in Sri Lanka similarly derives from the existence of the dominant Sinhala nationalism which sees itself as the guardian of Buddhist culture. Attempts by the non-Buddhist Tamil community to assert their rights were seen as an attack on the integrity of Sinhala identity. The violent reaction to Tamil civil rights protests in the late 1970s and early 1980s began a long cycle of violence lasting over two decades.

In contrast to 'solutions by violence' are 'solutions by compromise'. The situation in Switzerland provides an early example of the latter. The quality of 'Swissness' relates to a civic culture, and is underpinned by the equal status accorded each of the four languages of the state (German, French, Italian and Romanisch). This equality is enforced by the legal right of each Swiss citizen to insist on being addressed in any of the four languages by a public official.

In Canada, the Anglo-French linguistic conflict was resolved in the mid-1960s by the adoption of bilingual multiculturalism. This gave French (the language of the defeated colonists of 1759) equal status with English, the language of the victors. The policy was given constitutional status by the Multiculturalism Act of 1988.

The situation in the UK presents elements of these 'compromise' examples. Language rights have been given to the languages of the Celtic nations, but not to those of recent migrant communities. Anti-discrimination laws do not in themselves define permanent relationships between different communities. The exception is in Northern Ireland, where the Good Friday Agreement of 1998 led to legislation which defined and embedded the 'Two Traditions' (Unionism and Republicanism) in law and public policy. This unexpected outcome of the 30-year civil war in Northern Ireland demonstrates how the debate about multiculturalism is both ideologically fluid and in practical terms decisive for the immediate future of many countries.

Culture

Most debates on multiculturalism take place on the grounds of culture. In Europe and North America these debates are driven by the consequences of the post-1945 economic boom. This generated a demand for labour which in turn led to mass immigration from ex-colonial countries (in the case of former imperial powers) and from other agrarian-based countries (in the case of other industrialised states).

All these migrants carried their own social relations, traditions, religions and languages with them to their new homes. Whatever their original intentions may have been about length of stay, most became permanent residents and moved their families over to join them. During the 1960s, the advent of mass air travel meant that migrants were able to reinforce their traditions by constant visits to their original homes. By contrast, pre-1939 migrant communities gradually became divorced from their places of origin and as a result developed significant cultural differences from their home communities. This often meant losing their 'native' language after one generation.

Doubts are often raised over the level of legitimacy given to immigrant social traditions. This has been the source of bitter controversy in the USA ever since the arrival of large numbers of Irish immigrants in the 1840s. Supporters of an 'essentialist' view of American identity, which came out of a British 'Anglo-Saxon' heritage, viewed this and subsequent migrations as a fundamental threat to American identity. In the case of the Irish, it was both religion and language that were seen as problems. Language, however, has always been the most important point of contention in the USA. The American tradition has always seen the USA as a monolingual society and state.

Hispanic migration from South America in the late 1990s revived this issue. By the mid-1990s some counties in some US states had large Hispanic majorities. Spanish language radio stations sustained Spanish as a living language for these migrants, and fuelled demands to give the use of Spanish formal status in public life, most notably in Dade County (Miami), where some primary schools were 100% Hispanic. To counteract this trend, the Florida State Congress passed an act preventing the use of Spanish as a medium of instruction in public (state) schools.

Such identity politics are at the centre of debates about multiculturalism. They arise from the idea that distinct communities are the building blocks of societies. Each community is thought to possess its own unique and distinct features, and the multiculturalist implication is that each of these features is of equal moral value. This view is the basis of the sociological-political concept of pluralism. Each culture has the right of equal access to political power and to educational and economic opportunities. The state should act as the guarantor of these, and if necessary be the agency that provides them. The multiculturalist vision of society is one with no dominant culture and no single essential nature.

Originally pluralism was developed as a theoretical response to discrimination against the black citizens of the USA. However, the criteria used are so general that they can easily be applied to almost any distinct section of any population. The concept has facilitated the growth of a multitude of forms of 'particularism' — distinct ways of defining a community that set it apart from the rest of the population. Because it is easy to use, language has long been a common way of doing this. Ethnicity has provided another method of distinction; some groups in society share a common language and religion, for instance Christian English-speaking black Americans or Dutch Reformed Church Afrikaans-speaking 'Cape Coloureds' in apartheid-era South Africa.

In Europe religion has become the dominant issue over the last 20 years and, crucially, the position of Islam has created the most controversy. The issues arising from the Iranian Revolution of 1979, an overt fusion of politics, religion and state power, have been carried over into subsequent conflicts in the Middle East and Afghanistan. Since these conflicts have involved major Western powers, migrant communities of Muslim origin in Europe have become much more conscious of their Islamic nature. This process has been assisted by the funding of conservative Islamic groups in these countries by the Arab monarchies. Migrant communities have frequently developed much more conservative and 'particular' practices (over dress codes, for instance) than those practised in their countries of origin. The mirror image of this process has been the emergence of hostile movements inside the 'host' communities. These seek to defend what is perceived to be their own cultural identity, which is often a mixture of Christianity and twentieth-century secularism, frequently also expressed in terms of dress codes.

The recent focus on religion has only partially obscured an earlier conflict based more clearly on ethnicity. This conflict was sparked by the presence of large non-white migrant communities, with extreme right groups bitterly attacking these communities as the source of cultural and racial degeneration. This aspect of multiculturalism has not vanished in recent years, and is being revived because of the large contemporary migration of people from sub-Saharan Africa into Europe. Parties such as the BNP in the UK, for instance, are obsessed with the growth in the numbers of mixed-race citizens. However this issue is no longer in the forefront of public debate as it was in the 1970s; concerns about religion now dominate.

Minority rights

This concept grew directly out of pluralism. If all minority groups in society are of equal value to everyone else, then they must have equal rights. However, most minority groups have suffered discrimination for long periods in the past, usually on racial grounds. Because of this their position in society has invariably been that of a culturally dispossessed and impoverished force of manual labourers. They have usually lacked education, economic strength and political power. The promotion of equal rights has thus taken the form of redressing the balance and investing minority communities with the level of rights and opportunities expected by the rest of the population.

This approach first developed in the USA after the success of the Civil Rights Movement. It was quickly obvious that the Civil Rights Act (1964) and the Voting Rights Act (1965) would not in themselves deal with the problems of poverty faced by black Americans. The solution, successfully promoted by black pressure groups, was that of 'affirmative action'. This strategy demanded that public policy go out of its way to assist the development of communities that had suffered discrimination. It was justified on the grounds that without such action these communities could never assume their rightful place on an equal level with the rest of society. This strategy migrated to the UK in the 1970s (becoming known as 'positive discrimination'), and has been firmly embedded in British practice since the mid-1980s. Here, it primarily affects the behaviour and policies of local authorities and public agencies such as the NHS.

Minority rights can also apply to ethnic groups living in clearly-defined territories. Usually these are given to the earlier residents of states that were created by European settler colonies, such as in the USA (Native Americans), Canada (Inuit), New Zealand (Maori) and Australia (Aborigines). The rights conferred vary between countries, but all have proved to be controversial. They arise from a formal recognition that the colonial settlement was an act of aggression (and so probably a war crime under contemporary international law). Colonial settlement harmed the original communities and for this harm they are due both compensation and the granting of political authority. These moves have been criticised for undermining the fundamental legitimacy of the states concerned, seriously undermining their traditions and national identity.

All policies derived from the principle of minority rights can be subject to bitter criticism. Liberals attack them for imposing a collectivist view of the world on society. Individuals within these communities are forced into an identity that may have been chosen for them by self-appointed 'community leaders'. Liberals point out that there are serious disagreements over what constitutes a number of identities and that public bodies may make decisions about how to recognise what defines a community on the grounds of short-term pragmatism rather than principle. At worst, this may descend into opportunism, for instance by deferring to community leaders who are thought to be capable of delivering the most 'block votes'. Feminist campaigners against forced marriage and domestic violence frequently accuse public bodies of deferring to 'community cultural values' for fear of being accused of racism and discriminatory practices.

Another liberal criticism is that this collectivist view leads to the infringement of the freedom of speech. This criticism arose in response to the dispute about Salman Rushdie's book *The Satanic Verses* (1988), which was accused of being insulting to Islam. Liberals argue that all liberties are underpinned by the freedom of speech. Once that freedom is infringed all other liberties are at risk because there is then no end to the qualifications to liberty that can be made. Furthermore the Enlightenment principle of rational enquiry demands that nothing is exempt from the most searching scrutiny and bitter criticism. To allow any one religion to claim exemption from scrutiny is thus to undermine the fundamental principles of liberal society that have existed since the Enlightenment.

Minority rights have also been attacked for discriminating against the majority community. Critics dispute the allocation of public funds to minority community organisations and the allocation of resources such as social housing to recent migrants. Critics also argue that it leads to under-qualified people being appointed to jobs, which results in a lowering of the standards of public service.

Diversity

The celebration of diversity is a core feature of multiculturalism. In contemporary Britain public bodies are assessed by how effectively they promote diversity. Citizenship education places a central focus on diversity, and the legitimation of diversity in personal identity. On the other hand, diversity is criticised for undermining the homogeneity of the nation, and so promoting social tension and discord. Diversity is set against the preferred principles of integration (where migrants adopt the practices of the host community) or assimilation (where migrants are absorbed into the host community). In their different ways these two principles demand that immigrants have an obligation to adjust themselves to the practices of the host community and to obey its expectations of heritage and cultural norms.

This tension between diversity and integration exists in the USA. The motto of the republic is *E Pluribus Unum* — from many shall come one. This is a very ambivalent statement. On the one hand it can be interpreted as demanding that anyone wishing to become a citizen must adopt the principles of 'Americanism', sometimes called 'the American Way'. On the other hand, it can be interpreted to mean that migrants can forge a completely new, American, identity out of the acceptance of the universal principles laid out in the Constitution. In itself this does not preclude them from retaining a sense of where they came from, as long as they give pride of place to their 'Americanness'. This explains the existence of a diverse range of 'hyphen-Americans' — African-Americans, Italian-Americans, Asian-Americans and so on. As long as the 'native' identity is the adjective qualifying the American noun, this diversity is seen as not only acceptable but a particular strength of the American identity. This was precisely the point argued by President Obama in his inaugural address in January 2009.

The argument rests on the assumption that diversity is beneficial to society and the individual. It is said to bring an increasing range of experiences and cultural 'inputs' that greatly increase the scope of society. A frequent example is that of music and other forms of culture, which make a society more vibrant and also free modern mass society from the danger of developing the dull conformism that was warned against by philosophers such as John Stuart Mill (1806–73). Individuals also have their perception of the world enlarged by participating in a diverse society. The attainment of self-realisation is assisted by access to a range of ideas, philosophies and cultural experiences. It reduces the incidence of prejudice, which is typically generated by a lack of contact with other cultures and a literal ignorance of the nature of other people's cultures. Tensions and conflicts are said to occur rarely *within* areas of great diversity. Rather they habitually arise on the boundaries *between* areas dominated by different religious, ethnic or cultural groups. Sectarian conflict in Glasgow does not usually occur in social settings in the city centre, where people mix as anonymous individuals, but between different groups of supporters at Celtic-Rangers fixtures, where everyone is clearly defined by their team's colours.

Liberal multiculturalism

This political form of multiculturalism derives from the key liberal principle of tolerance. This says that all individuals possess equal worth, and therefore their ideas, religion, language and culture are of equal worth with any other in society. This is especially true of vulnerable people such as immigrants or asylum-seekers, and people should not attempt to force their ideas on these or any other groups in society.

The principle of toleration argues against the most extreme forms of integrationism and assimilation. The host society is not allowed to insist that new arrivals embrace every form of the host culture and identity. As long as all residents obey the laws of the land they have a right to practise their religion and foster their culture as they see fit.

Moreover liberals in the UK believe that, given an 'open society' offering freedom of expression, practices that might be seen as inadvisable will fall away as a result of competition from new ideas. This explains the often mutually incomprehensible attitudes adopted in the UK and France to the wearing of the hijab in schools by Muslim girls. In the UK it is regarded as a matter of individual choice, if taken as an autonomous decision by the individual. As long as it conforms to general regulations regarding school uniform and health and safety law then it is purely an issue of personal choice guaranteed by the principle of toleration. In France it is seen as a fundamental assault on the 'republican values' of the separation of religion and the state. The preservation of these values over-rides any issue of individual rights. Additionally, French liberals overwhelmingly assert that since the wearing of these garments is objectively symbolic of individual subservience to religion and of women's oppression, then the individuals concerned *cannot* be making a free choice.

This debate has exposed the serious tensions within liberalism: toleration cannot be extended to intolerant activities. This position is the liberal justification for the prohibition of acts of racial discrimination and of racially abusive language and publications. Similar hostility to practices judged to be intolerant is now being applied to a number of cultural practices in some migrant communities, for instance those surrounding marriage and dress codes, especially dress codes relating to women. Since the decline in the general use of 'demure' clothing — headscarves veils and long dresses — in Europe and North America since the First World War, an assumption has grown up that such clothing *must* be an expression of reactionary patriarchal values being imposed upon women. The attitude held by many liberals is that whatever people may do in their own homes (the 'private' sphere) in public life they have no right to impose anti-individualist practices. Since marriage, for instance, is a civil (and therefore a public) event as well as a religious one, no one has the right to impose anti-individualist practices (such as forced marriages) on anyone else.

Pluralist multiculturalism

Although it arises from within the liberal tradition, pluralist multiculturalism has developed beyond the boundaries of liberalism. It argues that there is no single route to an ideal life or form of society. This is frequently criticised as being 'moral relativism', meaning an absence of any absolute standards by which to judge behaviour. This can lead to any act being seen as legitimate, even if it violates the views of the overwhelming majority of the rest of society. It also implies that the liberal values of Western society no longer have universal application. In this line of thinking liberal values will have to exist as just another value system competing against authoritarian ideologies. The prospect is that liberalism will not be competing on very favourable terms outside its core base in Europe and North America.

Other views, such as those expressed by the UK academic Professor Bhikhu Parekh (b. 1935), argue that human societies are far too complex to have one unique set of universal values. In one sense this view is a reversion to Edmund Burke's image of society as being composed of distinct 'small platoons' — groups with their own history, rights and identities — although this now applies on a global scale.

Liberalism and its features of democracy and individual rights have long been criticised in Africa and Asia as examples of colonial domination. After independence most African states did away with multi-party parliamentary democracy. Where the new rulers bothered to make an argument for it that went beyond 'repressing tribalism' to ensure national survival, they did so on the grounds of reflecting the essential nature of African society. This was argued to be so different from that of Europe that different forms of political organisation were both legitimate and essential to ensure the stability of society. This was the argument put forward by President Julius Nyerere (1922–99) of Tanzania. There the concept of 'African Socialism' kept the principle of competitive elections within a single party state.

In South America liberal values, including property rights, have been criticised as being instruments used to maintain the rule of narrow, autocratic elites. These are said to be the agents of American and European business interests which have entered into an alliance to oppress the majority of the people. Liberation for the oppressed people must mean the overthrow of these universal values which have been hypocritically used to legitimise centuries of repression and dictatorship. This is one of the principles of the 'Bolivarian Revolution' in Venezuela and the 'indigenous' movements in other South American countries. They claim inspiration from and legitimacy for traditions that predate liberalism. This is a campaign for pluralist multiculturalism on a continental scale.

It is also possible to identify a form of 'particularist' multiculturalism. This states that diversity involves unequal power, and this inequality must be addressed. This leads to supporting 'affirmative action' of the kind mentioned above in relation to the USA and the UK. It is a way to formulate a theory of minority rights on a general, even global, scale.

Cosmopolitan multiculturalism

Cosmopolitanism is the process by which a large number of distinct cultures come into contact with each other, and in the process of so doing produce a culture that is different to any of them. In a sense this can be seen as the antithesis of multiculturalism, since at the end of the process there will only be a single culture and identity. However, for the fusion to occur the preceding cultures must be in place and capable of interaction with each other. To be effective, this diversity of cultures has to consist of (more or less) free and equal entities otherwise one culture would become dominant and simply swamp the others.

Cosmopolitans therefore insist on multiculturalism and diversity as a necessary precondition for the desired fusion to come about. The new culture will be the fruit of all the best of its source cultures, greatly expanded by their interaction. American multiculturalists point to jazz as the prime example of this process. As argued by the documentary film-maker Ken Burns in his series *Jazz* (2001), although jazz had clear African origins it could not have come into existence in Africa. It emerged from the interaction of African-American culture with a white culture seeking to free itself from its European heritage. It could only have been created in the USA, because it fitted the demands of that society for a 'truly American' music. While jazz was not what many white American cultural figures anticipated, it is a true example of a cosmopolitan culture and has been embraced across the entire range of the American population.

This image is very different from the alternative concept of 'pick and mix' multiculturalism. Here individuals make random cultural choices from a range of 'offers'. This refers to the extension of diverse food and culture choices, or, for example, the 'supermarket of religions' generated by New Age ideas. In other words, 'pick and mix' multiculturalism is a hybrid (it possesses the features of more than one identity) whereas true cosmopolitanism implies a totally new identity. Cosmopolitanism can be seen as another expression of the US motto *E Pluribus Unum*.

Criticisms of multiculturalism

Multiculturalism has been criticised from a range of ideological viewpoints.

Liberal criticism

Liberals have attacked its legitimacy because it is said to violate universal values. It promotes a collectivist image of society; individuals are only thought to possess an identity, and so only to have value, as members of a community. Liberals argue that this means that human rights, especially that of freedom of speech, are at risk. They point out that the desire to protect the dignity of the community has led to a number of campaigns against books and plays by 'community leaders'. These have had the object of silencing dissident members of the communities concerned. Liberals say that multiculturalism assumes that people have one single identity, which must determine their entire existence. Multiculturalism therefore gives opportunity and legitimacy to anti-liberal authoritarian ideologies, notably Islamicism, to make inroads into British society.

Conservative criticism

The conservative criticism arises from the threat that multiculturalism is seen to pose to the organic society. Conservatives say that the delicate balance of such organic societies that has been produced by centuries of history is being destroyed by the rapid entry of large populations who do not share national values. Possibly more crucially, they do not share the same historical experience; they cannot share the same heritage of the host population because their own 'narrative' (that which tells them who they are and how they became who they are) is essentially different from everyone else's. So it is impossible for them to identify with the national history and the national institutions.

For conservatives the issue is partly one of numbers; isolated individuals are little problem, since they can be absorbed within a single generation. More importantly it is an issue of the requirement to give equal moral value to the traditions and beliefs of immigrants. Doing so of necessity devalues the heritage of the host community. Feeling disinherited by the lack of respect given to their traditions, elements from the host community will react and social disorder will be the outcome. On the other hand, should the multicultural experiment succeed, the essential national identity will have been lost forever. Something of unique value will have vanished, impoverishing future generations and undermining crucial features of inheritance and tradition. Lacking these assets, whatever multicultural society comes into being as a result will be impoverished, weak and unstable compared to that which it has replaced.

Feminist criticism

Feminists have criticised multiculturalism for legitimising imported patriarchal values. Under the cover of the idea of 'respect for all cultures', oppressive practices such as forced marriage, domestic violence and female circumcision are allowed to exist, sometimes with the complicity of authorities who 'turn a blind eye' to activities that are against the law. This is why so many feminists pay close attention to the wearing of European dress as an essential feature of personal liberation. This kind of criticism is extended to other religions' attitudes towards gays and lesbians. It becomes the litmus test for international solidarity. Thus the US and UK governments attempted to justify intervention in Afghanistan after 2001 on the basis that it ensured freedom for women from reactionary and oppressive practices.

Socialist criticism

Multiculturalism has also been criticised from a socialist viewpoint because it marginalises class as a determinant of social progress. Identity politics have been criticised in general by socialists as diverting the working class from attacking economic exploitation. Socialists argue that multiculturalism can end up as little more than a celebration of the growth of a middle class from minority groups, or of the ascent of individuals into high positions in professional and political life. Socialists say that change is increasingly viewed on a community scale, leading to what has been termed a system of 'spoils democracy'. This is where electorates voting on ethnic or religious lines expect their representatives to deliver resources in the form of public jobs, contracts and development funds to their 'own' community. Rather than seeking change and the advancement of society as a whole, elected representatives of minority communities may merely attempt to use electoral success to obtain an increased share of existing resources. They then distribute these to their own 'constituency', hoping to ensure their continued political success.

Questions & Answers

This section of the guide looks at a range of answers to the type of questions that you will face in your Unit 4 examination. It is divided into two content areas: the short-answer questions in Section A and the essay questions in Section B. Within each of these sections there are two model answers for each of the ideologies. One of these is an A-grade and the other is a C-grade answer.

None of the answers is perfect. Each represents one way of approaching the question, with an indication of the grade that it might achieve.

Immediately after the question, before the student answer, you will find an examiner's advice section. This outlines the focus and scope of the question. Following each answer there is an 'Examiner's comment' (indicated by the symbol *e*). This deals with the main strengths and weaknesses of the answer. In the essay question answers you will also find shorter comments interspersed throughout the answer. These commentaries give you an indication of what is required to achieve an A-grade answer, and help you to become familiar with the three assessment objectives mentioned in the Introduction to this guide.

This guide is intended to help you to develop your skills and capabilities. It is better to attempt the questions *first*, and then read the student answers and the comments. You can then review your work in the light of these. The student answers are *not* model answers to be memorised and then repeated word for word in the examination. You are unlikely to be faced with these specific questions and there is always more than one way in which a comprehensive answer can be given to any question.

Section A

■ ■ ■

Nationalism

Distinguish between races and nations, and explain why these two terms have been confused. (15 marks)

✍ It is important to make clear distinctions here by stating that nations can be defined on non-racial grounds, before explaining how races have been defined. The second part of the answer should explain how right-wing nationalists usually define nations on exclusive grounds (which are frequently based on race, sometimes disguised as 'culture') rather than as civic entities.

■ ■ ■

A-grade answer

A nation is a group of people bound together by cultures and traditions that they have in common. Examples include language, traditions, dress, religion, ethnicity and history. This is very brief and will be examined more in depth after a brief definition of race. Race is a group of people bound by a common genetic inheritance, thus distinguishing themselves from others by biological factors. Examples of these different features are skin colour, height, and facial features.

It can be very difficult to distinguish between some nations. For example, Australians and New Zealanders speak English but would be horrified if they were classed as part of the English nation. This shows how nation can be a subjective term as it is very much left to the discretion of someone as to which nation they define themselves as belonging to.

Race, however, can be defined scientifically as it is through the science of genetics that it is determined. It is still easy to confuse races, though, as mixed race families become more common in a multicultural society. Does one class mixed race children as a new race or as a part of two races?

question

The two terms may easily be confused as they both have features in common despite the difference in definition. People from the same genetic inheritance will often have the same language, history, traditions, dress and religion, just as people from the same nation will often have similar skin colour, build and facial features.

To conclude, both nation and race are a means of classifying people, they are completely different methods but they have a lot in common. The main reason for confusion is that most people don't know the true definition of each term.

This answer scores well in the first paragraph. Here it clearly draws on the crucial distinction that while 'race' is based on objective genetic inheritance, 'nation' can be based on a range of definitions and gives a list of a number of the most frequently used criteria. The second paragraph brings out the way in which nation can be defined subjectively, and how the criteria (such as language) are not exclusive.

The attempt to explain confusion is much weaker. The paragraph on mixed-race people relates to confusion about race, not about confusion between race and nation. The next paragraph, while descriptively accurate, does not deal with the way in which confusion is created by the ideology of right-wing nationalism. However, taken as a whole this is a higher-level response to a difficult question.

For the level of knowledge demonstrated by this response, the examiner would award 4/5 of the AO1 marks (knowledge and understanding). For the quality of analysis, the examiner would award 5/7 of the AO2 marks (analysing and evaluating political information). For the quality of argument developed through the answer, the examiner would award 2/3 of the AO3 marks (constructing and communicating coherent arguments).

The answer would receive a total of 11/15 marks.

■ ■ ■

C-grade answer

The difference between races and nations can be viewed objectively by analysing their different features, and subjectively by analysing the ways that different ideologies view them.

Objectively, races are made up of different ethnic groups that share a common genetic origin, which cannot be changed and which is inherited from one generation to another. Nations are linked to a specific geographical area and can be made up of several races, like the USA. Their extent can change through border changes and migration.

Races and nations are often confused because they come to be associated with each other. Many people often refer to the oppression of Jews by Germans. Obviously many nations are composed of one majority race (Anglo-Saxons in England,

African-Caribbeans in Jamaica) and many minority races. The danger is that these minority races become ignored or worse, seen as external to the nation.

⟨e⟩ This answer makes a serviceable distinction between nation and race in the second paragraph, but it could have been further developed, especially the definition of a nation. The answer suggests a useful example for exploring the definition of a nation by raising the example of the USA. This could have led on to a short discussion of the nature of civic nationalism, but it is not followed up.

The final paragraph demonstrates a failure to understand what the nature of the confusion can be. It is presented as an argument about the dangers of racial oppression, not as an explanation of the confusion between nation and race.

For the level of knowledge demonstrated by this response, the examiner would award 3/5 of the AO1 marks (knowledge and understanding). For the quality of analysis, the examiner would award 3/7 of the AO2 marks (analysing and evaluating political information). For the quality of argument developed through the answer, the examiner would award 2/3 of the AO3 marks (constructing and communicating coherent arguments).

The answer would receive a total of 8/15 marks.

Feminism

Why do radical feminists proclaim that 'the personal is political?'   (15 marks)

e You need to explain why radical feminists think that gender divisions are the most important of all in society. It is then necessary to explain how these divisions are reflected by patriarchy in the private or personal realm. You should discuss how this leads radical feminists to see politics in terms of power-structured relationships, rather than as a public activity linked to control of governmental institutions.

■ ■ ■

A-grade answer

Radical feminists regard gender as the most important division in society, and see that women are oppressed and disadvantaged within society due to their gender difference. This difference needs to be overthrown, allowing women to achieve liberation from their gender, and hence emancipation and equality within society.

Radical feminists view society as having a hierarchical structure, characterised by patriarchy, as superiority of males and the subordination of females. Their view is that this patriarchy is evident within all male and female relationships, not just those in the outwardly political sphere. Indeed, their view is that patriarchy has its roots within the traditional family structure, and that patriarchy within society is a reflection of this.

Therefore in order for this patriarchy to be overthrown, and women liberated, relationships within the family must be changed, not just those within wider society. Radical feminists feel that by ignoring the state of relationships in the personal sphere the oppression of women has been ignored altogether. Therefore the barriers between the personal and the public spheres must be broken down.

In particular, they place an emphasis on the sexual and psychological oppression that women suffer within the domestic sphere. This is in contrast to the social oppression in the workplace, as they feel that the social situation will not be improved unless gender differences in the private sphere are resolved.

In order for women to achieve emancipation within the personal sphere, conditioning must stop and women must be educated to recognise the fact that human nature is androgynous. Firestone even went so far as to suggest that women could also be liberated from their biological sex differences by achieving the process of reproduction artificially, breaking down the traditional structure of the family.

e This answer shows a good understanding of the core relationships of women's oppression and how the private sphere underpins it. It explains how the family operates as an oppressive institution by noting that radical feminists think it influences all other aspects of life, without developing the point in full. However, the final paragraph does provide an explanation of the implication of the Women's Movement slogan ('the personal is political') that a sexual revolution is needed to overthrow and replace patriarchy.

For the level of knowledge demonstrated by this response, the examiner would award 4/5 of the AO1 marks (knowledge and understanding). For the quality of analysis, the examiner would award 5/7 of the AO2 marks (analysing and evaluating political information). For the quality of argument developed through the answer, the examiner would award 2/3 of the AO3 marks (constructing and communicating coherent arguments).

The answer would receive a total of **11/15 marks**.

■ ■ ■

C-grade answer

Traditionally, politics has been only concerned with the public sphere (e.g. political parties and government policies), not the private sphere (e.g. childcare and marriage). Gender stereotyping says that women's natural place is in the home, and not with politics.

Radical feminists say that formal legal and political equality is not enough. Equal pay has not created equality with men in the home or in relationships. Equality of opportunity in the public sphere, for instance in employment, has not tackled the most oppressive institution of all — the family.

To achieve equality women need radical action, to revolutionise cultural, political and family structures. Kate Millett argues that this should be done by women living in women-only communes. Germaine Greer in *The Female Eunuch* argues that this should be done by having sexual equality also.

To achieve equality and liberation women need a sexual revolution that will totally transform their social relations. They need to become 'women-centered' and reject the patriarchal family and everything that it represents. Some radical feminists argue for 'political lesbianism', a complete severing of all social relations with men.

🖉 This answer lacks a definition of women's oppression and patriarchy. This would have given greater impact to the first two paragraphs, which are clearly relevant to the question, and are by far the strongest part of the answer. Thereafter the answer begins to drift away into describing various remedies to women's oppression which are not clearly related to the question that has been asked.

For the level of knowledge demonstrated by this response, the examiner would award 3/5 of the AO1 marks (knowledge and understanding). For the quality of analysis, the examiner would award 3/7 of the AO2 marks (analysing and evaluating political information). For the quality of argument developed through the answer, the examiner would award 2/3 of the AO3 marks (constructing and communicating coherent arguments).

The answer would receive a total of **8/15 marks**.

Question 3

Ecologism

Why do some conservatives support ecologism? (15 marks)

Here you must clearly explain the reasons why different conservatives support ecologism. You must differentiate between the supporters of different sub-traditions, especially traditional conservatism and neo-liberalism, who adopt very different arguments for supporting ecologism. You should also address the 'some' aspect by noting why conservative support for ecologism may be limited.

■ ■ ■

A-grade answer

Conservatives support ecologism for a number of different reasons. Very reactionary conservatives look back to an ideal society that is almost medieval in its nature, and certainly one that is predominantly agricultural. Such people dislike modern society and everything that it has produced and so want to prevent it encroaching on what remains of 'the natural countryside'.

More mainstream traditional conservatives want to maintain what has been handed down from earlier generations. They view the environment as an inheritance that we have a duty to transmit to our descendants. The environment is not something that is there for the current generation to mine for its own use with no thought for future impact. Such conservatives will be in favour of conservation measures for natural resources such as fish stocks, and in restricting urban expansion.

Some neo-liberal conservatives support a form of 'green capitalism'. They are worried that the depletion of the environment by unrestrained economic expansion is a form of 'market failure' that will quickly undermine the existence of the market itself. They therefore support measures such as carbon trading to deal with climate change as a way of bringing about the necessary changes.

It is important to note that these ideas are all forms of 'light green', or 'shallow ecological' ideas. Almost no conservatives see humans as a fundamental threat to nature and they think that humans are the most important part of the natural world.

This answer addresses a range of conservative approaches to ecologism. It clearly distinguishes two arguments: the traditional and neo-liberal conservative reasons for supporting ecologism.

While these points are well made, the answer does not explain why conservative support for ecologism is limited. This could have been done in the final paragraph, by explaining how conservatives are fundamentally opposed to the basic principles of deep ecology, which demand a complete change in the nature of society. A complete answer would have (briefly) explained how deep ecology contradicts basic conservative assumptions of the value of inherited traditions and institutions. For neo-liberals, deep ecology is a threat to the free market and to capitalism.

It would have been more useful for the issue of extent to be mentioned in the first paragraph rather than the final one. Discussion of the issue of why some conservatives do not support ecologism would then have been an obvious and natural way to complete the paragraph.

For the level of knowledge demonstrated by this response, the examiner would award 4/5 of the AO1 marks (knowledge and understanding). For the quality of analysis, the examiner would award 6/7 of the AO2 marks (analysing and evaluating political information). For the quality of argument developed through the answer, the examiner would award 2/3 of the AO3 marks (constructing and communicating coherent arguments).

The answer would receive a total of 12/15 marks.

■ ■ ■

C-grade answer

Conservatives support ecologism because they believe in preserving traditional ways of life and the countryside that supports them.

They believe that we have a duty towards future generations to preserve the environment, and a duty to our forefathers to preserve what they have handed down to us. Because they want to preserve society they are in favour of measures to save the countryside from being built over, and to keep endangered species from being made extinct. Therefore, conservatives oppose such measures as the new runway for Heathrow Airport. This is because it will destroy established communities.

Conservatives are also worried that the destruction of the environment may destroy the economy. Environmental degradation produces huge economic costs through pollution and climate change that could cause huge economic problems in the future. That is why some conservatives support actions to deal with climate change and support green policies such as recycling.

Not all conservatives support ecological policies. Some conservatives are closely attached to industrial interests such as oil firms. These people see ecological policies as a threat to their businesses and so oppose measures that will limit their growth. Some others think that ecologism is a threat to tradition.

🖉 This argument tends to treat conservative ideas on ecologism as a single 'job lot'. The first two paragraphs cover the traditional and neo-liberal approaches without explicitly recognising them. The 'traditional' argument is the best developed because it does explain a theoretical reason for support for ecologism, and gives a relevant contemporary example. The 'neo-liberal' paragraph could, but does not, mention the role of the market in its approach to the two examples given.

The final paragraph gives an instrumental rather than an ideological reason for why some conservatives oppose ecologism. The final sentence states an ideological criticism, but does nothing to explain it.

question

For the level of knowledge demonstrated by this response, the examiner would award 3/5 of the AO1 marks (knowledge and understanding). For the quality of analysis, the examiner would award 3/7 of the AO2 marks (analysing and evaluating political information). For the quality of argument developed through the answer, the examiner would award 2/3 of the AO3 marks (constructing and communicating coherent arguments).

The answer would receive a total of 8/15 marks.

Multiculturalism

Why do liberals both support and criticise multiculturalism? (15 marks)

ℰ Here you need to make sure that you answer both aspects of the question. Liberal multiculturalists focus on the need for toleration, which is based on the principle of individual freedom. This principle is also the main reason why some liberals oppose multiculturalism, on the grounds that it leads to the imposition of group identities on individuals. You will need to explain how liberals can reach such opposed conclusions on the basis of the same principle.

■ ■ ■

A-grade answer

Liberal multiculturalists support multiculturalism because they believe in toleration. For them, all ideas, religions and cultures are of equal value. Individuals have the right to pursue whatever religion or culture that they wish. This is the most important human right. Any attempt to force anyone to give up any part of their culture is oppressive.

Liberals also believe that everyone benefits from having a range of cultures in a society. Because they do not believe that any culture, or people, has the monopoly of truth or positive features, they think that everyone in society gains from being in contact with a wide range of different cultures. They point to the positive impact that different music cultures have had on each other in recent times as an example of this.

However, some liberals are very hostile to multiculturalism. They say that it imposes a collective identity on individuals. People are seen as members of groups rather than as individuals. They say that in practice multiculturalism means supporting 'community' values above everything else, and ignoring those individuals in these communities who want to deviate from given norms.

This comes out particularly in relation to issues like forced marriages. Anti-multiculturalist liberals say that authorities such as police and local councils have not supported victims of forced marriage and domestic violence among minority communities because they are worried about being accused of being racist. They say that this means abandoning the universal value of human rights (of women in these cases) and giving in to 'cultural relativism'. This means accepting that there are no absolute values but values which apply differently in different communities.

So liberals are deeply split over whether multiculturalism supports or threatens the rights of the individual.

ℰ This answer attempts to provide a balanced response. The first two paragraphs cover the main reasons for liberal support of multiculturalism: toleration and the benefits to society of diversity and cultural exchange. The point on toleration could be extended by a discussion of why liberals think it wrong to impose your ideas on others, and why a 'free market of ideas' may bring rational humans closer to the truth. However, this is a competent explanation of the pro-multicultural argument.

The next two paragraphs give the core arguments by liberals who are hostile to multiculturalism, raising the points of collectivist conformism, and the ways in which multiculturalism is seen as providing legitimacy for illiberal practices. A closer command of formal vocabulary (such as by constantly using the term 'collectivism' to contrast with 'individualism') would have made it easier for this candidate to have expressed his or her points more effectively.

For the level of knowledge demonstrated by this response, the examiner would award 4/5 of the AO1 marks (knowledge and understanding). For the quality of analysis, the examiner would award 6/7 of the AO2 marks (analysing and evaluating political information). For the quality of argument developed through the answer, the examiner would award 2/3 of the AO3 marks (constructing and communicating coherent arguments).

The answer would receive a total of 12/15 marks.

■ ■ ■

C-grade answer

Liberals support multiculturalism because they believe in individual freedom. For them, freedom is the most important thing of all. Just as individuals should be free to do anything that they like, as long as it does not restrict anyone else's freedom, communities should be free to practise their own religions and way of life.

Like Rousseau, liberals say 'I disagree with what you say, but I will defend to the death your right to say it'. This means that they will tolerate views and practices that they do not agree with. This is because to try to suppress these ideas would need an oppressive government, which liberals are completely opposed to.

Some liberals oppose multiculturalism because various communities have practices which restrict the freedom of individuals. Many religious groups are hostile to gay rights, for example. Liberals support gay rights because of their belief in personal freedom, and so some liberals think that multiculturalism means giving credibility to anti-liberal ideas, and holding back the struggle for individual freedom.

Therefore liberals both support and oppose multiculturalism. They cannot agree on whether it promotes or hinders the development of individual freedoms and so often seem to be confused about whether it should be supported.

🖉 This answer recognises the demands of the question and attempts to address both parts. While the information the candidate gives is in the main creditable, he or she does not develop or explain the points made. The first two paragraphs state basic liberal reasons for supporting multiculturalism, but do not explain why these are valuable features.

The candidate could have mentioned, for instance, that individual freedom allows people's personalities to develop to their full potential, and that this will benefit all of society. Toleration develops the best qualities of the people who are being tolerant, so societies where different groups are tolerated are the most pleasant to live in.

The paragraph on why some liberals oppose toleration mentions one relevant criticism of multiculturalism but fails to develop a full range — for instance attitudes towards women or the role of religion in society.

For the level of knowledge demonstrated by this response, the examiner would award 3/5 of the AO1 marks (knowledge and understanding). For the quality of analysis, the examiner would award 4/7 of the AO2 marks (analysing and evaluating political information). For the quality of argument developed through the answer, the examiner would award 2/3 of the AO3 marks (constructing and communicating coherent arguments).

The answer would receive a total of 9/15 marks.

Section B

*In Section B you have to answer **one** essay question from a choice of three. This means that one of the ideologies will not have an essay question set in each examination. It is important to understand that there is no set rotation for specific ideologies to appear in this section. You must prepare for the examination on the basis that **any** three could appear.*

The questions in this section examine major issues concerned with the ideologies. They will require you to discuss differences and similarities between the various versions of the ideologies, and come to a reasoned judgment on the question asked.

Remember that there are 12 marks for AO1 (knowledge), 24 marks for AO2 (analysis and evaluation) including 12 marks for synopticity, and 9 marks for AO3 (communication), a total of 45 marks.

■ ■ ■

Nationalism

To what extent is nationalism inherently expansionist? (45 marks)

🖉 This is not a 'for or against' question. A comprehensive answer requires that you discuss the full range of the various forms of nationalism, from liberal nationalism with its aspects of universal 'brotherhood of nations' and post-1945 anti-colonial nationalism, to conservative forms of nationalism and the aggressive, racially-based nationalism associated with Nazi Germany. Having discussed the relationship of these different forms with expansionism, you should then make a judgement on how far it is appropriate to characterise nationalism as a whole as expansionist.

■ ■ ■

A-grade answer

To describe nationalism as inherently expansionist is to ignore the different forms of nationalism that exist. Expansionist nationalism can be said to feature aggressiveness and therefore destructiveness. However, there must be a proper appreciation of liberal nationalism, which preaches quite the opposite to expansionism. It extols the virtues of toleration and pluralism and peace between nations. This proves that nationalism is not necessarily destructive.

Expansionist nationalism can be said to have a link to ethno-cultural nationalism, which practises exclusivity and is wary of any outside influences or 'alien' existence within nation. It can be said to believe in racial purity and have contempt for any move towards racial dilution or mixing, so in this sense Hitler can be said to have displayed elements of expansionist theories. This adoption and insistence on racial and ethnic purity can have severe implications for the society without and within. If expansionist nationalists are hostile towards any different people, this can pose a problem for world peace, as this type of nationalism when confronted by outside forces or forces that are different from within, responds with aggression, national chauvinism and so forth. This in turn can be destructive and threaten world peace causing international anarchy.

Expansionist nationalists are typically intolerant of any differences that may exist within their nations. This can be seen by Hitler's goal to expand Germany and make it the most forceful and important power in the world, by eliminating any different people inside Germany that he thought stood in the way of the expansion of the German nation. He found the differences within the nation particularly threatening to the nationhood and this was reflected in his programme of anti-Semitism, which carried out awful atrocities such as the persecution of each and every Jew in sight and herding them into concentration camps where they would be killed.

Expansionists see the nation as organic. This view was supported for instance by Mussolini's belief in society being an organism and that individuals work for the sake of the organism and not in their own individual interests. He thought that individual interests should be dissolved into the whole and even be sacrificed for the sake of the whole. This view is potentially destructive as the individual's beliefs or interests are not regarded and if there is strong opposition to the nation's beliefs or actions then individuals will be annihilated as seen in Hitler's annihilation of the Jews as they supported genuine democracy.

Liberal nationalists, however, can be said to be inherently peaceful and harmonious. They advocate an inclusive nation which embraces different types of people. Race, religion and gender are irrelevant so long as a 'general will' is adopted to abide by the nation's actions and authority. This can be reflected in nation-states such as the United States of America, which has a diverse mix of people from culturally varied backgrounds. This can be said to promote social and cultural pluralism. The liberals regard the nation as a 'voluntaristic' association of people, based on people's citizenship as opposed to their descent. Individuals within a liberal state have a degree of civic loyalty as it is a voluntary association, therefore the individual is more likely to share the same will as the nation.

Liberal nationalism believes in peace between nations and has taken a cosmopolitan approach to international relations. In its extreme form, this means the embrace of all humanity in a world nation-state. However, in moderation it focuses on peace and harmony between states and nations, and believes that nationalism does not necessarily have to mean intolerance between nations, but can make room for differences in cultures and political beliefs. Liberal nationalists believe that cultural and political diversity only enriches international society as opposed to causing it to be degenerate.

It is not possible to state that nationalism is inherently expansionist and destructive as there are different forms of nationalism, such as liberal nationalism, which has links with the idea of a civic nation which is pro-internationalism and pro-globalisation,

which leads to interdependency, therefore making it impossible for a war between nations, and is therefore not destructive in nature.

This able candidate has suffered because he or she has not focused on the precise question that has been asked. The answer would have been much better had the conclusion been written as the introduction. The candidate would then have been able to direct the answer to addressing the question asked.

Instead, far too much time and space is spent on describing key features of the two kinds of nationalism referred to, without establishing any clear relation of these features to the central issue of expansionism. Much of what is written is implicitly relevant, but not in a way that can be given much credit. The diversion into description means that the candidate omits to mention two important sub-traditions, conservative and anti-colonial nationalism, both of which are relevant to the question.

Having said all this, when the candidate does come back to the question of expansionism there is much relevant, well-explained information, especially in the discussion of the internationalist aspects of liberal nationalism. These sections rescue the answer, and would be given enough credit to place it in the lower reaches of the grade range.

For the level of knowledge demonstrated by this response, the examiner would award 8/12 of the AO1 marks (knowledge and understanding). For the quality of analysis, the examiner would award 8 of the AO2 marks (analysing and evaluating political information) and 7 marks for synopticity out of a total of 24. For the quality of argument developed through the answer, the examiner would award 6/9 of the AO3 marks (constructing and communicating coherent arguments).

The answer would receive a total of 29/45 marks.

■ ■ ■

C-grade answer

Nationalism has been described as a 'chameleon' ideology, because it is perhaps the most versatile of all political ideologies. It has also been one of the most influential over the past century, causing wars, revolutions, the redrawing of national boundaries, the collapse of empires and the birth of states. However, this diversity brings into question whether or not nationalism can be considered expansionist because there are distinct differences between the four main strands: liberal nationalism, conservative nationalism, chauvinistic nationalism and anti-colonial nationalism.

Nationalism's major ideal is that of the nation — a collection of individuals who may share similar ethnicity, territory, history, language or religion, and whose goals are to preserve their interests. This may be by creating their own nation-state or by being within another sovereign country.

Liberal nationalism focuses on tolerance, and the rights of nations to self-determination. This doctrine can be split further into two major components: the political and cultural spheres, where the former seeks some form of political independence (e.g. in Scotland), while the latter seeks to preserve a nation's language and traditions (e.g. in Wales). Liberals have traditionally been ambivalent towards nationalism because of its aggressive character, which may impinge on an individual's personal rights and freedoms. Also it can lead to aggression by bigger nations against smaller ones, which goes against the principle of self-determination.

Chauvinistic nationalists believe that humans are governed by will and support struggle and war. Recent examples include Mussolini's fascist regime as well as Hitler's Nazi Germany. These regimes believed in a hierarchy of nations, and thus sought to create an empire and world domination. This contrasts with the liberal view of individual rights against the elitism and racism of the chauvinists.

Conservative nationalism grew out of the need for social cohesion and the need to celebrate a national ideal during times of great hardship, such as the two World Wars. It also focuses on the perceived threat of globalisation, supranational bodies as well as localism and regionalism. It seeks to unite its citizens by reflecting on tradition.

Anti-colonial nationalism has virulently anti-Western ideals. It rejects Western colonialism and preaches national independence. It has often been united with socialist elements, such as those in many African regimes.

Thus there are numerous contradictions within nationalism which means that it is not always expansionist. Nationalism can be progressive or reactionary and expansionist, it can advocate tolerance or war, so that although it has some common threads it is not always expansionist.

🖉 This answer shows that the candidate understands the question and there are some points of merit in parts of the answer. However, the first two paragraphs simply describe features of nationalism, and do not begin to address the question that has been asked.

The paragraph on liberal nationalism begins and ends by addressing the question, but in the middle it veers off into another description of features that do not in themselves refer to the key issue of expansionism. It implies that liberal nationalism has transferred concepts of human rights to nations, but never directly makes that point or develops it.

The paragraph on chauvinist nationalism comes closest to answering the question as it directly discusses expansionism. Again there is little explanation of the concept of the nation that was embodied in fascist Italy or Nazi Germany that led to the aggressive expansionism associated with both states.

The paragraph on conservative nationalism does not address the question at all, while that on anti-colonial nationalism does so extremely briefly, missing the opportunity to explain how it is by nature the complete opposite of expansionism and rejects the expansionist theory that other nations are not fit to rule themselves.

The conclusion is not an evaluation of the discussion, but a repetition of the main points of the essay.

5

question

For the level of knowledge demonstrated by this response, the examiner would award 6/12 of the AO1 marks (knowledge and understanding). For the quality of analysis, the examiner would award 6 of the AO2 marks (analysing and evaluating political information) and 6 marks for synopticity out of a total of 24. For the quality of argument developed through the answer, the examiner would award 5/9 of the AO3 marks (constructing and communicating coherent arguments).

The answer would receive a total of 23/45 marks.

Feminism

Why is there a liberal and socialist feminism, but no conservative feminism? (45 marks)

This answer requires you to deal with both the overlaps between feminism and the other ideologies, and the extent to which contradictions exist. With liberalism and socialism you will be expected to identify the significant common features as well as points of difference, while with conservatism there may be little scope for compatibility given the basic feminist critique of existing society.

■ ■ ■

A-grade answer

Feminism is a varied political doctrine which has showed many different faces, mainly those of radical feminism, liberal feminism and socialist feminism. Although no strand of conservative feminism exists, this doesn't mean to say that to a minor extent some feminist ideas could not have a degree of compatibility with conservatism.

The core belief of feminism is that gender differences between men and women have a negative impact upon women in society, and hence should be diminished, so that women can achieve emancipation. The doctrines of liberalism and socialism have both managed to use that belief and adapt it in different ways, suggesting different goals.

Liberalism is compatible with feminism due to the fact that liberals have a very strong concept of individuality that leads them to believe that all individuals, despite being different, are entitled to equal rights, opportunities and standing in law. Women should be entitled to these rights of individuals in the same way as men, as J. S. Mill pointed out in *On the Subjection of Women*. Hence gender differences should be minimal in order to give men and women equal standing. However, in line with the concept of individual freedom that is important for liberals, they do not believe in intervening in the 'personal sphere' of domestic life in order to eradicate these differences. Indeed, they maintain that men and women may have different inclinations within the family, but that this should not mean that women suffer political inequality. Although they do not therefore take the extreme viewpoint of feminism, feminist ideas are clearly compatible with the liberal doctrine.

Socialists however have objected to the oppression of women as they see it in tandem with capitalism, and aim for a social revolution in which both are overthrown. The oppression of women works to the benefit of capitalism, as women constitute a reserve workforce who are only used when it is convenient to do so, and bear and rear children in order to allow the continuation of the male workforce. Thus by overthrowing gender differences, the main goal of socialist feminists is for women to be equal in economic terms to men, being given the same wage for labour and treated equally within the workplace. However, while social democrats have advocated class and gender divisions as equally important, Marxists have emphasised that people

should focus to a greater extent on class divisions, as gender is not the most significant social difference to address. Thus although one may face difficulties in attempting to hold both Marxism and feminism as of high importance, generally speaking feminism is compatible with socialism.

Conservatives traditionally view society as being organic and naturally hierarchical. Thus they accept the oppression of women and superiority of men as a natural social divide that should not be interfered with. Thus the view is that patriarchy should be maintained as opposed to being overthrown, and the uneven relationship between men and women is seen as a natural security for society rather than a point of conflict.

However, in principle conservatives do believe to an extent that individuals are born with equal moral worth (foundational equality), and that they deserve equal opportunity. Thus although wanting hierarchy to remain, one could suggest that they may accept to a degree a slightly watered down version of liberal feminism, whereby women are treated equally under the law. This would especially be true of conservatives today, as society as a whole has come to accept the idea that women and men are legally equal. Although liberal feminist ideas may not have been accepted by early twentieth-century conservatives, there would be few conservatives today willing to question the idea that women should not have the vote. However, it is unlikely that any form of conservativism would be likely to associate itself with radical attempts at emancipation.

Difference feminism could also be said to have a degree of compatibility with conservatism, as both advocate that gender differences to an extent are natural. They both see that men and women have different inclinations, and so women should not attempt to become equal with men. However, the conclusions held by difference feminists are often extreme and advocate separation between the sexes. Conservatives would not agree with this, as they see that the patriarchal relationship between men and women is a source of harmony, not of conflict.

Therefore to conclude, feminism is compatible with many political doctrines, including that of conservatism. However, there is more affinity between feminism and liberalism and socialism than there is with conservatism.

This answer provides a good treatment of all the different aspects required by the question, rising to a very good treatment of feminism's relationship with conservatism, where it successfully qualifies the assumption contained in the question.

The section on liberal feminism identifies the core liberal concept of the sovereign individual as the basis of the positive relationship with feminism. It mentions the tension related to liberal feminist reserve over the 'public–private' divide, but this could have benefited from further explanation.

The paragraph on socialist feminism identifies the key aspects, such as the reserve army of labour concept. The section on Marxism and feminism could have been rounded out by a reference to Engels' work on the role of property in the subjection of women.

The section on conservatism identifies the central conservative criticism that feminism is incompatible with the concept of the organic society. It then, by implication, discusses how, on the basis of pragmatism, conservatives can accept some changes achieved by feminism (the point could have been made more briefly had the term been used), and then points out the partial overlap between some of the ideas of difference feminism and conservatism.

The conclusion merely summarises the points already made, and the lack of an effective evaluation of the overall argument holds it below the very highest level of marks.

For the level of knowledge demonstrated by this response, the examiner would award 10/12 of the AO1 marks (knowledge and understanding). For the quality of analysis, the examiner would award 10 of the AO2 marks (analysing and evaluating political information) and 10 marks for synopticity out of a total of 24. For the quality of argument developed through the answer, the examiner would award 7/9 of the AO3 marks (constructing and communicating coherent arguments).

The answer would receive a total of 37/45 marks.

■ ■ ■

C-grade answer

Feminism takes many forms and has many subdivisions, so it can be compatible with other ideologies, notably liberalism and socialism. Conservatism, however, is an ideology which advocates traditional values and feminism, as a modern and progressive school of thought, is difficult to associate with it.

Liberal feminism has been the most mainstream of feminist philosophy, and initiated the movement in the eighteenth century with Wollstonecraft's *Vindication of the Rights of Women.* Her book was written at a time when women had few rights in comparison with men, not being allowed to vote, or even own property when married. Wollstonecroft argued that women had the same faculties of reason as men, and should therefore have the same political status and same liberties as men. This coincided with liberal ideas of human rationality and the innate equality of humankind. Liberalism followed feminism to its first wave in the early twentieth century with the demand for women's right to vote, which they fully achieved in 1928. The second wave of feminism demanded equal opportunities for women in the public sphere, so that women could achieve the same power and status as men. This liberal feminism was based on liberalism's idea of equality of opportunity, breaking down the barriers of society, or in the feminists' case, patriarchy.

Conservatives have criticised feminism for endangering the natural state of the family by seeking equal status with men. The belief in the traditional role of the woman as the domestic creature, with the raising of children as a priority is favoured by many conservatives, so for them liberal feminism threatens the natural order of society.

Feminism's support for the choice of abortion has upset and infuriated many Christian conservative groups and the neo-conservatives in the USA, whose politics are very moralistic and often based on religious values. The sexual liberation of women and the increasing openness of female sexuality is also upsetting for the neo-cons who see promiscuity as a threat to family values.

Conservatives see society as successful organism that has been passed down the generations and is based on a natural 'order' of existence. All kinds of feminism challenge this natural state of affairs, and conservatives believe that this can only bring conflict and social breakdown. Therefore they believe that feminism threatens the wellbeing of society.

Another branch of feminism is socialism. It is concerned with the economic and social welfare of women as a priority over women's equal opportunities. Issues such as pay differences, rape and brutal oppression in African and Middle Eastern countries are important to socialist feminists. This branch of feminism is highly incompatible with conservatism as it seeks to reform society.

It seems that feminism, despite its diversity, is highly incompatible with conservatism as it is progressive, whereas conservatism tends to be reactionary.

🖉 This is an example of a very uneven answer that fails to meet all the demands of the question. A further consequence of this failure is that the candidate is unable to provide an effective evaluation at the end of the essay, producing an extremely brief conclusion that does not even summarise the arguments that have been made.

The section on liberal feminism is by far the strongest, but even this tends to become descriptive when talking about 'second wave' feminism. To be complete a discussion on liberal feminism needs to mention the fact that it does not recognise the 'private sphere' as an arena of gender conflict.

The section on conservatism is poorly structured. Theoretical points and description are mixed together in a way that does not deploy them to their best effect. The final point on the organic society as a fundamentally conservative criticism should have been placed first, which would have enabled the candidate to use the other points as explanation and development.

The last paragraph on socialist feminism simply describes a couple of its concerns, and offers none of the socialist feminist criticisms of capitalism as the source of gender inequality.

For the level of knowledge demonstrated by this response, the examiner would award 7/12 of the AO1 marks (knowledge and understanding). For the quality of analysis, the examiner would award 6 of the AO2 marks (analysing and evaluating political information) and 6 marks for synopticity out of a total of 24. For the quality of argument developed through the answer, the examiner would award 4/9 of the AO3 marks (constructing and communicating coherent arguments).

The answer would receive a total of 23/45 marks.

Ecologism

To what extent is ecologism a rejection of all other ideologies? (45 marks)

This question demands a balanced answer. This entails a recognition that ecologism is not one single undifferentiated ideology. You will have to discuss how 'deep' and 'shallow' ecology have different attitudes towards other ideologies because of their different views on the role of nature and the position of humans in relation to other species. These different attitudes produce two different strategies: 'dark' and 'light' green policies. The former are very difficult to accommodate to other ideologies, while the latter have proved to be compatible with significant parts of several ideological traditions.

■ ■ ■

A-grade answer

There are two aspects of ecological ideas: deep ecology and shallow ecology. These give rise to different types of solutions: dark green and light green policies. These two approaches have very different attitudes towards other ideologies.

Deep ecology is very critical of most other ideologies. It accuses them of 'anthropocentricism' — seeing human life as the reason for all other existence. Deep ecologists see the world as being a single interdependent ecosystem, as in James Lovelock's 'Gaia' theory. Therefore they regard humans as just one part of existence, with no priority rights over other species in a claim on the earth's resources. Deep ecologists claim that most other ideologies are guilty of promoting industrialism. They say that this creates a never-ending drive for economic growth that is destroying the planet through pollution, the destruction of natural habitats, and the production of climate change.

Deep ecologists argue for radical policies to create sustainability for human society. They wish to reduce the impact that humans have on the planet by cutting back on levels of economic activity. They wish to reduce international air travel and trade and, most controversially, to reduce global population drastically. They want to do this because they think that it is humanity which is the greatest danger to life on the planet because it has the desire and capacity to expand its 'needs' almost indefinitely. Their ideal is a non-industrial world, with most people living in small self-sustaining communities.

These ideals are totally hostile to most other ideologies. Conservatism, liberalism, and socialism all put humans at the centre of their ideas. Conservatives certainly see human society as being the pinnacle of creation (if they are religious), or at the peak of evolution (if they are not). Liberals believe that there is nothing that rational humans cannot come to understand, and there is no problem that they cannot solve. Socialists share that view, but also believe that there is no basic conflict between humans and other species. Problems are only caused by capitalism, which drives a wedge between

humans and the natural world in the interests of selfish and destructive ruling classes. Once capitalism has been overthrown and equality established human society can be brought back into harmony with nature.

The one ideology that does overlap with deep ecology is eco-feminism. This is a version of radical feminism which believes that patriarchal society is responsible for environmental destruction, because it is the male desire for domination that drives men to separate themselves from nature. Once patriarchy has been overthrown and women are able to reassert their natural instincts for living in harmony with nature, society will be transformed. The male desire for mastery of the world will be replaced by a rejection of consumerism and a desire to return to a simple life in partnership with nature.

In contrast to deep ecology, shallow ecology does not try to transform society. Shallow ecology takes humanity as its starting point and aims to make changes that will make it possible to preserve existing society in a viable form. To this extent it is possible for it to coexist with elements from each of the other main ideologies. It promotes modest, 'light green', solutions that can be implemented by existing national and international bodies. The Kyoto Protocol on climate change is an example of this, as are the fishing quotas imposed by the European Union.

This approach is obviously compatible with liberalism and socialism. Both of these ideologies see humans as rational beings who have the ability to make objective decisions about the greater good, and can make plans for effective changes. Both ideologies support international action to preserve natural habitats such as the rainforests, and governmental policies to reduce carbon emissions to combat climate change.

Some conservatives can also support a number of 'light green' policies because of their ideas about the nature of society. They see society as an 'organism', where all the parts of this body need to be healthy so that the body can survive. So if any part becomes diseased and cannot function properly it has to be healed. Such conservatives see environmental problems as a 'sickness', and so measures to heal them are justified and necessary. Some conservatives also believe that because of the principle of inheritance we have a duty to pass on the functioning world we inherit to our descendants. Environmentalism also fits well with the very traditional 'pastoralist' wing of conservatism, which is hostile to industrial society and idealises pre-industrial agriculturalism.

🖉 This answer recognises that there is a debate to be had over the issue raised in the question. The candidate understands that ecologism is not a single undifferentiated ideology, and that attitudes towards other ideologies have to be viewed through the different perspectives of deep and shallow ecology.

The paragraphs on deep ecology provide a core explanation of the principles of deep ecology, and then show how, by not placing humans at the centre of their ideas, deep ecologists are at odds with the other main ideologies. While the candidate could have developed a discussion on sustainability at this point, (which would have shown how deep ecology rejects all forms of economic development) the essay does provide a clear explanation of the principle areas of incompatibility. It also recognises, in the paragraph on eco-feminism, that not every ideology is uniformly hostile to deep ecology.

The second part of the answer demonstrates how shallow ecology, with its focus on humanity, has a very different attitude towards other ideologies. The candidate develops this theme with reference to the aspects of the three core ideologies which are compatible with the ideas of shallow ecology. The conclusion reinforces the rest of the essay, by recognising and summarising the crucial point that it is the differences inside ecologism that create its relationships with other ideologies.

For the level of knowledge demonstrated by this response, the examiner would award 10/12 of the AO1 marks (knowledge and understanding). For the quality of analysis, the examiner would award 10 of the AO2 marks (analysing and evaluating political information) and 10 marks for synopticity out of a total of 24. For the quality of argument developed through the answer, the examiner would award 7/9 of the AO3 marks (constructing and communicating coherent arguments).

The answer would receive a total of 37/45 marks.

■ ■ ■

C-grade answer

Ecologism is opposed to other ideologies because all the others are committed to industrialism and economic growth. They all support humans' rights to deplete the planet's resources for their own use. Ecologism disputes this idea, holding that all other living beings have equal rights with humans, and the planet itself, as a living biosphere, has its own rights.

Ecologism accuses other ideologies of being guilty of anthropocentricism — of seeing humans and their needs as being more important than any other living things. Because of this they are willing to allow fragile ecosystems to be disrupted for short-term economic gains. An example of this is the cutting down of the Amazonian rainforest to enable the cultivation of soya and the raising of cattle. This will have very serious affects on global climate, but Brazilian governments of all ideological descriptions have allowed the destruction to proceed.

Conservatism is especially guilty of anthropocentricism. Most conservative ethics place humans at the centre of creation. Religious conservatives see humans as having been created in the image of God, and therefore they have the right to use the rest of creation for their own benefit. This is why the Bush administration passed laws allowing mining and logging in American wilderness areas. Even non-religious conservatives see humans as being so superior to other creatures that their needs should take precedence over those of other living things. They will always support animals being used for the benefit of humans, such as in medical testing and in factory farming. New Right conservatives believe that the free market will solve all problems, and so there should be no limits on business activities no matter what their impact on the environment.

Ecologists think that liberalism is almost as hostile an ideology as conservatism. Because liberals believe that humans are rational beings and capable of understanding anything, they support the growth of industry because they think that science and technology can solve all problems. They do not understand that it is science and technology, produced by rational humans, that is a large part of the problem. It has led to humans being separated from nature and thinking that they can safely remodel the world for their own benefit. Ecologism argues that humans must get back in touch with the rest of nature to survive. Humans have to realise that they are not separate and superior to the rest of the natural world, but are simply one small part of existence. Liberals will not accept this, because of their belief in individualism.

Ecologists think that socialism is as bad as all other ideologies. Despite being very critical of the effects of capitalism on the environment, they still want to expand industry and human consumption. They think that after the overthrow of capitalism they will still want to expand the human standard of living, which means more goods. This is shown by the way in which Communist countries such as the Soviet Union created environmental disasters with polluting industries. It poisoned huge areas of land in Central Asia with artificial fertilisers and almost drained the entire Aral Sea in order to provide irrigation for cotton plantations. It was Communist ideology that drove them on to do this. Ecologists do not believe that humans can 'conquer nature' in this way, unlike Communists. We are too weak to do this, but communism proves that we can despoil it for ourselves and for every other living thing.

So we can see that the other main ideologies are all hostile to ecologism. Because they all legitimise human actions to use nature for their own benefit, they will always be rejected by ecologism. Ecologism puts nature at the centre of its thought and wishes to change human society drastically so that it is not concerned with its own desires for increased consumption but with the wellbeing of the entire planet.

🖉 This is an example of a polemic: the candidate has allowed his/her own personal views to drive out a reasoned discussion and has ignored the existence of any counter-arguments. This is a serious risk when answering questions on ideologies.

In ignoring counter-arguments, the candidate has made the mistake of treating ideologies as undifferentiated entities. This is especially true of ecologism. All through the essay the candidate employs an essentially 'deep ecological' definition, although even this has not been fully developed. There is no recognition that there is another tendency (shallow ecology), which has a very different attitude towards other ideological traditions. The answer also fails to recognise differences within these other traditions. For instance, it is not true that all conservatives support factory farming — traditional pastoralists oppose it, for instance. The polemical approach inevitably leads to these sweeping (and inaccurate) generalisations for each ideology. Many socialists always were deeply critical of the policies of the Soviet Union that eventually produced environmental disasters. Not all liberals support the unrestrained development of industry.

This polemical weakness is unfortunate, because parts of the answer show significant understanding when dealing with each major ideological tradition. The critique of the religious new right, of liberal sympathy with science and technology, and with the Stalin-era Communist idea of conquering nature are all important points which have their place in a complete answer to this question. However since the essay at times reads like a speech for the prosecution rather than a discussion, these ideas are not fully developed.

The conclusion gives a very condensed version of the deep ecological position regarding the other traditions. The answer is not without some merit, but has not provided anything like a comprehensive answer to the question asked.

For the level of knowledge demonstrated by this response, the examiner would award 7/12 of the AO1 marks (knowledge and understanding). For the quality of analysis, the examiner would award 5 of the AO2 marks (analysing and evaluating political information) and 6 marks for synopticity out of a total of 24. For the quality of argument developed through the answer, the examiner would award 5/9 of the AO3 marks (constructing and communicating coherent arguments).

The answer would receive a total of 23/45 marks.

Multiculturalism

To what extent is multiculturalism hostile to conservatism? (45 marks)

A comprehensive answer to this question requires an initial discussion of the aspects of the two ideologies that may be in conflict, such as the nature of society and of rights, and in regard to tradition. However, it is essential to remember that to make a judgement answer 'how far' you will need to discuss those aspects where conservatism may have some compatibility with some features of multiculturalism. It is important to remember that there are a number of aspects of multiculturalism — it is not one uniform set of ideas.

■ ■ ■

A-grade answer

On the face of it multiculturalism and conservatism are polar opposites. The former is usually understood to mean acceptance of diversity and change in society. The latter stands for tradition and for continuity. However, not all types of conservatism are equally hostile to change.

Multiculturalism is based on the idea that all cultures are unique and are embedded in the histories of specific communities. The identity of individuals is shaped by the various aspects of culture such as language, religion, law and social customs, especially those that relate to the family. This idea can have a conservative aspect, as traditional conservatism sees all these factors as being parts of the make-up of 'organic society'. Social conservatism based around the patriarchal family is one of the aspects of minority ethnic communities that conservatives find most attractive. Some conservatives see these features of multiculturalism as an opportunity to 'roll back' the moral permissiveness that has undermined society since the 1960s.

For conservatives, problems arise when multiculturalism undermines fundamental features of society, such as the predominance of Christianity and the central place of the national language. Conservatives see the objectionable aspects of multiculturalism as those which place the cultures of minorities on an equal footing with those of the previously dominant majority. They think that this will upset the delicate balance of society that has worked well for centuries and could lead to disorder and conflict.

Conservatives are very sceptical about the multicultural principle of diversity. They do not believe that it necessarily brings strength to society. The conservative principles of prescriptive authority and obedience are based on the idea of political unity. This implies the acceptance of a single point of authority and an over-riding loyalty to the state. This goes back to Hobbes' vision of the need for an absolute power to keep a society from self-destructing. While this idea, and that of an integrated or 'organic' society, does not necessarily exclude the possibility of a very diverse society, in practice diversity has meant attempting to incorporate immigrant groups from other societies. For conservatives this raises the problem that these groups may bring in other existing loyalties with them, which they will not abandon just because they now live in another country.

Some conservatives see this as being a particular problem with the Muslim community. Some Muslims take the position that they have a primary loyalty to the international Islamic community (the Ummah) and this negates any demands of their new state for loyalty. Many conservatives say that promoting diversity has legitimised these anti-state attitudes, and has undermined the integrity of society by allowing a hostile body to flourish within it. They argue that unless these situations are rapidly brought under control they are likely to produce social conflict, as the 'disloyal' sections of the minority communities clash with hostile sections of the majority community.

Many conservatives follow this up by arguing that multiculturalism is an attack on the traditions of society. Conservatives see tradition as an essential 'social glue', which also gives people a sense of security and of 'place' within society. In countries such as Britain and France, with an imperial history, multiculturalism means accepting the permanent immigration of large populations from former colonies. Conservatives think that multiculturalism is a form of 're-writing' history by criticising the imperial past. Instead of empire builders being seen as heroes who brought civilisation and good government to the colonies, conservatives claim that multiculturalism portrays the imperial past as one of aggression and oppression, and the empire builders as little better than war criminals.

Even worse, this re-writing of history robs the indigenous population of pride in their own past and in effect leaves them adrift. They are put in the position of having to apologise in their own country for the supposed crimes of their own forefathers. Conservative critics say that this is not only unjust but it will also create social conflict as members of the indigenous community react against this process of 'historical evisceration'. They will fight to reclaim their own past against the multicultural views held by minority communities and which are being supported by the state. For conservatives, history should be written to reflect the traditions and views of the dominant, majority, section of society.

Neo-liberals from the New Right, however, have many fewer problems with multiculturalism. This is because they view society on a purely individualist basis, through the operation of the free market. For them what is important is the nature of individuals, and how they function in the market as rational beings. As long as people accept the free market as the basis of society it does not matter what their social origins, religion or cultural practices are. In fact, neo-liberals see all kinds of social discrimination and prejudice as forms of market dysfunction. They wish to see the maximum diversity of participation in the market so that there will be the greatest supply of entrepreneurial talent. This is why there are increasing numbers of young entrepreneurs from ethnic minorities. Of course, you could argue that the free market is itself a specific uniform type of culture, so that neo-liberalism is in fact the opposite of diversity.

On balance we can see that many of the different forms of conservatism are very sceptical, to say the least, about multiculturalism. They see all kinds of threats to authority, tradition, and to the organic society. This hostility is qualified by approval of the social conservatism inherent in many migrant communities, and by the compatibility of diversity and social equality inherent in neo-liberal conservatism. However, neo-liberals only accept diversity on an individualist basis, and so even this liberal attitude is hostile to the collective aspects of multiculturalism.

This answer attempts the full range of the question. The candidate discusses the core reasons for conservative unease about multiculturalism: the impact on social stability, on tradition and on the organic society. However, having mentioned the example of France, he or she then missed out on an opportunity to extend the discussion through a consideration of the French state's hostility to multiculturalism and its insistence on integration through the acceptance of 'republican values' such as the separation of religion and the state (recently highlighted by the controversy over the ban on the wearing of clothing with religious significance in schools). This would have given the candidate an opportunity to contrast multiculturalist and integrationist ideas. The candidate could also have recognised that multiculturalism is not only concerned with immigrant communities but also with sections of society that may have been present for many centuries.

However, the essay does provide a sound discussion of several conservative criticisms and discusses two areas where both traditional and New Right conservatives can come to terms with multiculturalism. In this way the candidate is able to show his or her recognition of a level of ambivalence in conservative attitudes, and explain this, providing an effective summary in the conclusion enabling the essay to achieve the top grade.

For the level of knowledge demonstrated by this response, the examiner would award 9/12 of the AO1 marks (knowledge and understanding). For the quality of analysis, the examiner would award 9 of the AO2 marks (analysing and evaluating political information) and 9 marks for synopticity out of a total of 24. For the quality of argument developed through the answer, the examiner would award 7/9 of the AO3 marks (constructing and communicating coherent arguments).

The answer would receive a total of 34/45 marks.

■ ■ ■

C-grade answer

Multiculturalism is hostile to conservatism because it is against tradition. It believes that all immigrant communities have the same rights as the indigenous population and so there should be positive discrimination to improve their position. This will mean that the nature of the country will have to be changed.

Tradition is very important for conservatives. They think that it is one of the main factors keeping society stable and that gives it legitimacy. Multiculturalism gives special rights to minority groups, especially immigrant ones. It promotes positive discrimination, which is a way of removing disadvantages that have been created by prejudice and discrimination. This can mean giving funds to these groups to promote their own communities and cultures, and by giving them preferential treatment in employment. It also means giving them a special place in education, for instance by celebrating their religions and festivals in schools and by teaching their languages and history.

All this goes against conservative ideas because it will gradually change the traditions of the country. Children will no longer grow up seeing Britain as a Christian country and English as its mother language. They will not learn about the important parts of British history. Conservatives think that this will not only change traditions but will also weaken the bonds that tie the organic society together.

Multiculturalism also clashes with conservatism because of its toleration of 'non-British' practices. This means not abiding by the 'cultural norms' of society, the informal rules that everyone obeys. These include respect for the law and all kinds of authority, and putting the welfare of society before that of your family or community. Conservatives argue that immigration has meant importing alien practices into British society. These include social practices such as forced marriage and religious practices such as a belief in witches and possession by the devil. These beliefs lead people from minority communities to think that they have the right to break the law. Conservatives say that multiculturalism has encouraged these practices because it argues that all cultures are equally valid and must be given equal respect. This has hampered the authorities in dealing with these illegal practices.

In this respect conservatives also point to the practice of 'block voting'. In Britain you are supposed to make up your mind individually and then cast your vote in a secret ballot. Conservatives say that in many migrant communities voting is decided on a family or community basis and then everyone is told who to vote for. The new postal voting system has helped this approach because many ballot papers can now be filled in by one member of the family. This belief in the 'block vote' has led to massive fraud in some areas where many false names have been registered as voters and ballot papers have been filled in by the supporters of candidates.

In general conservatives see multiculturalism as a threat to established society and to everything that they believe in. All the traditional features of British life are being changed by immigration and by the giving of equal status to the minority communities. The way that the country looks and sounds has been changed so much over the last 50 years that many old people feel that they are living in a foreign country. Food, music and clothes have changed drastically in that period because of immigration. Most importantly for conservatives, multiculturalism is reducing the respect held for the most important institution in the country, religion. Christianity and the Church of England (which is the official state church) are seen by conservatives as being the absolute core of society and national identity. This foundation is being undermined by the multiculturalist idea that all faiths have equal value and should be put on an equal footing. Even the Prince of Wales has said that when he becomes king he will

be the 'defender of faith' rather than the 'Defender of *the* Faith' as it says on the coins. To conservatives this is abandoning everything that has kept British society united and stable and must lead to disorder and conflict.

So in conclusion there is no way in which conservatism can accept multiculturalism. The ideologies are completely hostile and have opposing views of an ideal society. There is permanent conflict between them.

This is another example of a candidate answering a question using the assumption that an ideology is an undifferentiated block of ideas. There is no acknowledgment in the essay that there is any ambivalence at all in conservative thought towards any aspects of multiculturalism. This leads to a semi-polemical approach, which in a number of places reads like a reproduction of sensational articles from conservative sections of the media.

This approach creates a disjointed structure as if the candidate is remembering everything that he or she has read that was hostile to multiculturalism and then attempting to relate it to basic conservative ideas. This in turn leads to a failure to achieve command of knowledge. For instance, the paragraph on electoral fraud adds little of value to the answer, if only because concern over 'block voting' is not confined to conservatives; it is perhaps more of a worry to liberals since it offends their basic individualist and constitutional values. The penultimate paragraph, when it discusses religion, fails to acknowledge that a state church exists only in England, which seriously undermines its main argument.

However, the essay does discuss many points that are made by ideological conservatives against multiculturalism, and so notes a number of points of merit, even if they are not fully explained using the appropriate academic terminology. It therefore, somewhat fortuitously, manages to gain a C grade.

For the level of knowledge demonstrated by this response, the examiner would award 7/12 of the AO1 marks (knowledge and understanding). For the quality of analysis, the examiner would award 5 of the AO2 marks (analysing and evaluating political information) and 6 marks for synopticity out of a total of 24. For the quality of argument developed through the answer, the examiner would award 5/9 of the AO3 marks (constructing and communicating coherent arguments).

The answer would receive a total of 23/45 marks.